VENETIAN
TASTE

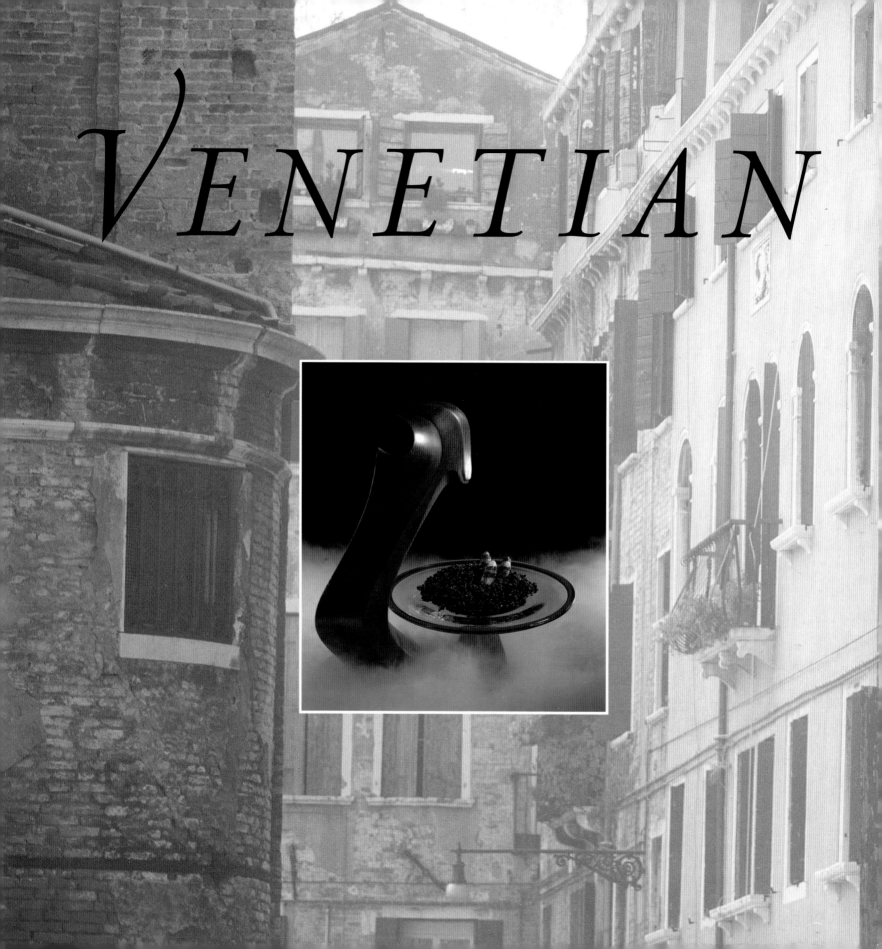

VENETIAN

TASTE

Created by ADAM D. TIHANY

Recipes by FRANCESCO ANTONUCCI

Text by FLORENCE FABRICANT

Food Artist: NIR ADAR

Photographer: PETER PIOPPO

ABBEVILLE PRESS PUBLISHERS

New York London Paris

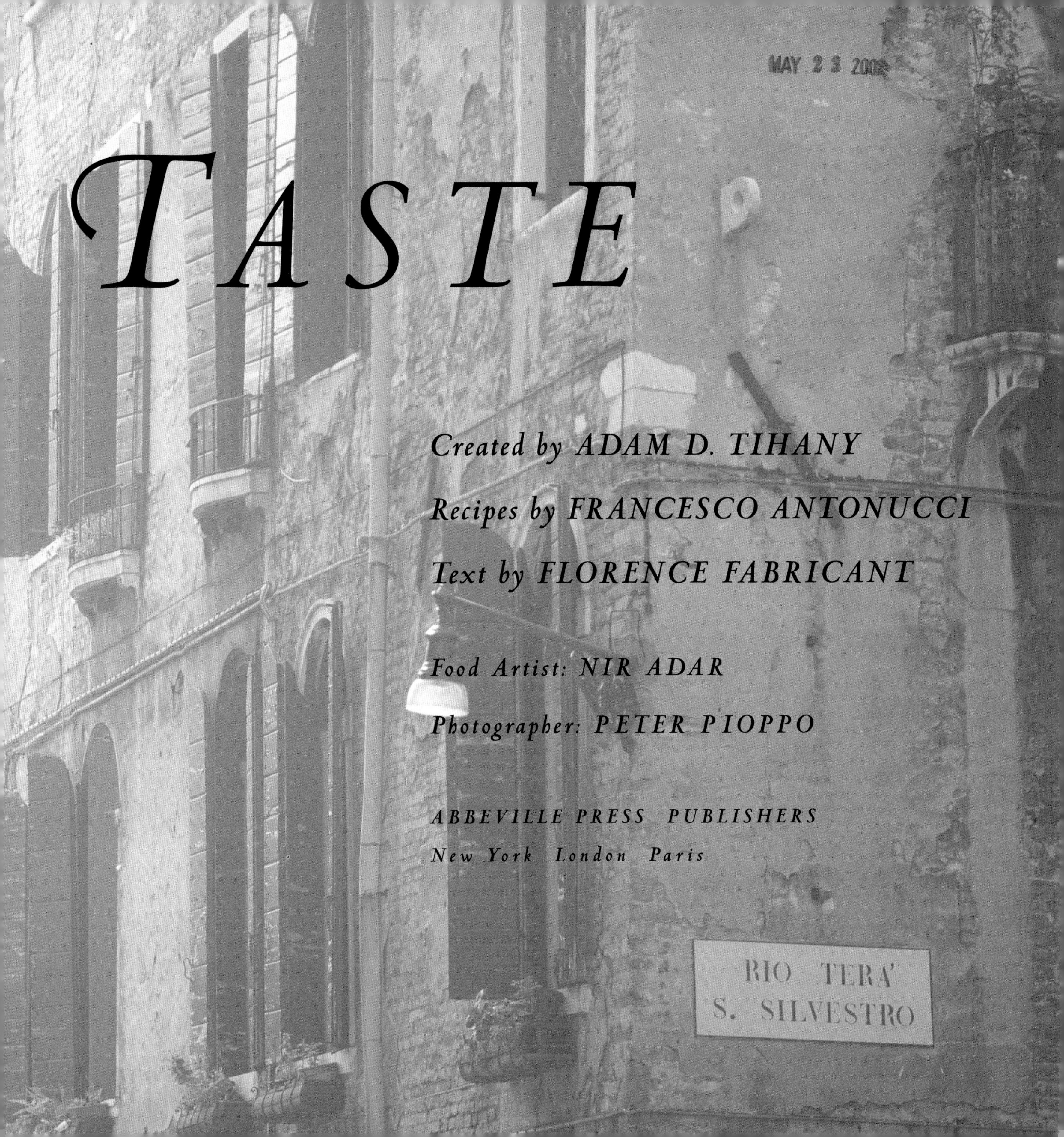

RIO TERA'
S. SILVESTRO

Front jacket: Tuna Carpaccio, recipe on page 45
Back jacket: top, A gondolier gracefully navigates his craft;
center, glassware in Carlo Moretti's studio on Murano;
bottom, a luncheon buffet given by Luciano Vistosi
Page 2: Black Risotto, recipe on page 62
Page 6: Tuna Ravioli with Ginger Marco Polo, recipe on page 81
Page 10: Gondolas are hitched to such gaily striped posts as these in front of
the palazzo Cavalli Franchetti along the Grand Canal.

Editor: Susan Costello
Designer: Patricia Fabricant
Production Editor: Abigail Asher
Text Editor: Virginia Croft
Production Manager: Simone René

First edition

Library of Congress Cataloging-in-Publication Data
Fabricant, Florence.
Venetian taste / created by Adam D. Tihany ; recipes by Francesco Antonucci ;
text by Florence Fabricant ; photographer : Peter Pioppo ; food artist : Nir Adar.
p.   cm.
Includes index.
ISBN 1-55859-548-1
1. Cookery, Italian—Northern style.   2. Cookery—Italy—Venice.
I. Tihany, Adam D.   II. Title.
TX723.2.N65F33   1994
641.5945—dc20   94-6993
CIP

To the Magic and Beauty of
Jacopo, Bram, and Sarah Venezia

A·C·K·N·O·W·L·E·D·G·M·E·N·T·S

"*Mille grazie*" to the wonderful Venetians, because without their help, we would still be attempting to unravel the mysteries of Venice:

Adriana and Luciano Vistosi, Natale Rusconi, Fred Laubi, Stefano Baccarat, Marcella and Victor Hazan, Fausto Maculan, Sandro Scarpa and his brothers, Carlo Moretti, Giuseppe Antonucci, Monica Pugiotto, Maurizio Billi and Luigino Vianello.

Our special thanks to the Remi–New York Venetian team:
Karl Tscholl, Jacobo Gusman, Christopher Gargone, Laurie Alleman, Augustin Pena and Dario Plozer, Javier Perea, and Tammy Meltzer.

And to Mania Hruska, whose friendship and wisdom helped Adam understand and love the Italian people.

To Jenifer Harvey Lang, without whom this book still would be just a dream.

We also wish to express our gratitude to the Abbeville team for its many contributions to this book, including Robert E. Abrams, Alan Mirken, Susan Costello, Patricia Fabricant, Abigail Asher, Virginia Croft, and Simone René.

C·O·N·T·E·N·T·S

Fegato alla Veneziana, recipe on pages 132–133

F·O·R·E·W·O·R·D

". . . in my opinion, if the earthly paradise where Adam dwelled with Eve were like Venice, Eve probably would have had a hard time to tempt him out of it with any fig. For it would have been another matter to lose Venice, where there are so many lovely things, than to lose that place where there are nothing but figs, melons, and grapes."

Pietro Aretino (1492–1556)

As anyone who has ever been truly in love with a city like Venice knows, the only way to share the experience is to take someone special by the hand and patiently and lovingly explore and savor the beauty, the secrets, and the rich unforgettable flavors.

Famous for centuries, Venice's courts, piazzas, theaters, coffee houses, and restaurants and even her dank alleyways and shadowed canals have attracted visitors from all over the world eager to taste of her culture. Lovers of the unusual, of exquisite detail, mysterious beauty, and complex flavors have flocked to Venice, drawn by her art, music, artisanry, and gastronomy and also bringing their own contributions to enhance her complex splendor. The city has absorbed all this, layer upon layer, century after century, to emerge a glorious and undisputed universal attraction that constantly eludes definition.

Like others who have come under her spell, I have found Venice to be a major source of inspiration. Her rich history, evident even in the most trivial detail of Venetian everyday life, has always stimulated my creative process. Every trip to Venice adds another meaning to the word "style" in my life, not to mention a couple of pounds—deliciously acquired—to my body. To help me share this love affair with you, Francesco Antonucci, my partner, who is a great Venetian, as well as a chef, opened his recipe book and heart; and together with friends like Florence Fabricant, Nir Adar, and Peter Pioppo, we created this book for all of you to enjoy.

Come, join us on this journey over water and experience the magic of "Venetian Taste"!

Adam D. Tihany

V·E·N·E·T·I·A·N T·A·S·T·E

Venice, La Serenissima, once supreme in its world, is ever sublime. This floating tapestry of 117 islands, a fantasy of lacy bridges and shrouded alleyways, of gilded palaces and dark canals, of romance and mystery, of fleeting images and lingering reflection, is a city of mists and sunshine that exists at the mercy of the moon-driven tides.

At one time the most important place on the planet, a crossroads for traders and travelers between east and west, north and south, it remains the most magical. In Lord Byron's words, "As from the stroke of an enchanter's wand: The revel of the earth, the masque of Italy!"

This fabulous realm that used sequins for currency, as if at a party, was governed by aristocrats of mercantile disposition, whose turn of mind was so pragmatic that they also invented the stock exchange. In addition they controlled the quality of the rest of Europe's food. The allure of the East appealed to the Venetian taste for the extravagant and was irresistible to Marco Polo, who embodied the essence of the adventurous, inquisitive Venetian spirit.

Venice became a place of mystically glittering Byzantine mosaics, serpentine arabesques, fantastic color, and, above all, a panoply of rich and exotic flavors.

In this vibrant kingdom that enjoyed independence for one thousand years, a cuisine of similar distinction evolved. And today, in a world of disappearing cultural borders, the delicately forthright cooking of Venice and style of presentation retain their uncommon character.

Venice is, above all, a proud city of the sea. In that shadowy time between ancient Rome and medieval Europe, the city's first settlements were on the beach at what is now the Lido. The early Venetians lived in a fragile water-bound fortress to protect themselves from predatory hordes on land. As the populace grew, so did the settlement and its power.

The Venetians began trading in salt and fish, built their boats, and from the 10th century on, under the leadership of successive doges (dialect for "leader," *dux* in Latin, *duce* in Italian), expanded their sphere of influence first toward Byzantium to the east, then to the Levant to the south, and eventually overland in Italy and the rest of Europe. The Adriatic became Venice's second lagoon.

To their commerce in salt and fish, the intrepid Venetians added a priceless catalogue of spices: pepper, ginger, saffron, cloves, and nutmeg. Then sugar brought from India and refined in Venice enriched the city's coffers as it sweetened the food of all Europe.

A fleet with ships built in the dockyards of the

St. Mark's in the sun

A shadowy canal

Arsenal made war to advance mercantile ambitions. Venetians joined the Crusades from the 12th to the 14th centuries, primarily because they understood that commerce could develop along the route rather than because of religious fervor. In fact, Venice was the only city-state in Italy never to submit to the control of the pope. "Venetians first, then Christians" (*veneziani, poi cristiani*) was the saying.

Venice's independent spirit, supported by its power, gave it the determination to resist the advances of the Turks, the Milanese, the Vatican, and the French and also made it a haven for political exiles from the internecine feuds in Florence and other provinces. Visitors like Jacopo d'Albizzotto Guidi, who came from Florence in 1427, described the fruiterers, poultry merchants, butchers, and wine sellers along streets also filled with goldsmiths, embroiderers, and vendors of tapestry.

The city was at a pinnacle of wealth and influence in the 15th century. Though it had lost some of its possessions in the Aegean Sea to the marauding Turks, Venice was still flourishing by the dawn of the 17th century, when John Evelyn, an English visitor, described it as "one of the most miraculously placed of any in the whole world, built on so many hundreds of Islands, in the very sea, and at a good distance from the continent."

Within one hundred years, having been embroiled in costly wars with the French, Spanish, and resurgent Turks, the republic had relinquished much of its empire. "The great days of Venice are over," said the French ambassador in 1718, after a peace treaty ending the War of the Spanish Succession was signed. "The city, however, remains a perpetual delight."

Throughout the 19th century, a time of occupation first by Napoleon, then by Austria, Venice continued to fascinate artists, writers, and musicians, who by 1846 could travel by train across the new bridge from Mestre on the mainland. Just as the complex harmonies of Vivaldi, the glowing artistry of Bellini and Titian, the theatricality of Goldoni and the Carnevale, and the imagination of such writers as Casanova were nurtured in Venice, the pens of others, like Ruskin, Browning, Sand, Mann, Proust, and Hemingway, and the brushes of Turner and Sargent would similarly be inspired. Its artistic wealth was eventually enriched by the long-term residence and legacy of Peggy Guggenheim in the 20th century.

Although Venice no longer boasted a huge merchant fleet, it turned to the wealth of its glass and gold, to tourism and fishing, activities it maintains with renewed vigor today.

Even without the might of a far-flung empire, Venice still depends on the bounty of the sea. Its cuisine not only is based on seafood but also celebrates the abundance of market gardens on outlying islands, farms of the hinterlands, and curiosities from around an expanded world that are constantly brought to its kitchens. And as only the Venetians can, they flavor all this with millennia of dra-

matic, luminescent history, with spices and herbs from afar, and with the shimmering inspiration of its water and light.

Here polenta is the color of saffron and rice is tinted with the ink of cuttlefish. Flower blossoms are fried or candied and eaten for their color as much as for their elusive, faintly aromatic flavor. Scents of ginger, nutmeg, mace, licorice, tarragon, and even curry tease in countless dishes. Ethereal dessert is fancifully dubbed "pick-me-up." The haunting dark fragrance of coffee perfumes the air.

Fish is central to the table. Little birds are preferred to larger game. Meat comes in translucent, saline slices of prosciutto, the rosy transparencies of carpaccio, or stir-fried slivers of *fegato alla veneziana*, a classic of Venetian cuisine that says it all: Asian stir-fry sweetly flavored with caramelized onion and edged with a touch of acid.

The bitterness of radicchio, the sweet and sour of

Setting hooks, plying the canals, and unloading wares at the Rialto market

many marinades, the pungency of olives and anchovies, are all part of the Venetian table. But there is always a lightness, a refusal to mask with heavy sauces, an insistence on freshness and balance, that dignifies the cuisine.

Venice was an early laboratory (and warehouse) important in the development of fine European cooking. Venetian merchants introduced such now-basic ingredients as sugar, rice, and coffee to the continent and long held a monopoly on the distribution of salt and pepper. If the morsels of food in a dish like *fegato alla veneziana* were bite-size, they were not cut small just to enhance the cooking, but to allow the fastidious Venetians to pick them up with their forks at a time when the rest of Europe was still licking its fingers. Forks and glassware were first used on the Venetian table. By the 16th century the cuisine was renowned throughout Europe for its delicacy. The artistry of thousands of unnamed craftsmen working in silk, lace, and lustrous glass has shaped the Venetian table.

The first Venetian cookbook, a six-volume work by

A mariner's legend in mosaic

Bartolomeo Scappi, was published in 1610. A Venetian of the period, Gerolamo Zanetti, compared the cooking of France unfavorably with that of his own city, writing that "French cooks have ruined Venetian stomachs with sauces, broths, extracts, meat and fish transformed to such a point that they are scarcely recognizable."

Tourists today are often surprised at the simplicity of the food and at the similarity of menus from restaurant to restaurant. While revelers at Carnevale go about disguised as birds and mountebanks, the cuisine does not stoop to artifice for flavor. Ultimately the food of Venice comes to the table embellished and distinguished, ever so subtly, by Byzantine, Turkish, Dalmatian, Persian, Spanish, Jewish, Austrian, Indian, African, and even Chinese notions.

Venetian food is not the cooking of Venice alone. There are three "Venices" that look to the city. Venezia Euganea, the area more often known as the Veneto, with Venice as its capital, extends from the gulf of Venice westward to the Lake of Garda and includes the cities of Padua, Verona, Vicenza, and Breganze. Treviso, a beautiful city of villas north of Venice, is also in the Veneto and shares the cuisine of seafood, grains, and vegetables.

In Cortina d'Ampezzo, the ski resort in the Dolomites where the Veneto stretches to the Austrian border, the food is rustic and more Germanic than Italian, as it is in the neighboring province of the Alto Adige, also known as Venezia Tridentina, situated between the Veneto and the borders of Austria and Switzerland. Here dumplings replace gnocchi, slabs of pork sausage fortify the polenta, and bollito misto anchors the main course. If there is fish, it is likely to be mountain trout. Strudel graces the dessert table.

To the east of Venice lies Friuli, or Venezia Giulia, where the sea marries hearty mountain cooking. Potato soup, roast pork, and cabbage dominate the table in the northern part of the region, while at lower elevations and nearer the sea, artichokes, asparagus, and seafood reappear. Like the Veneto, Friuli is known for its wines.

In the world of contemporary cuisines, regional cooking everywhere is being eroded by tides of trendy notions. The delight and surprise of seasonality have fallen victim to technology and global marketing. But the food of the Venice region continues to celebrate market freshness. While maintaining its tradition of fusing and interpreting many influences, it has also managed to sustain a unique, intriguing, and often seductive simplicity.

The Venetian table is essentially a frugal one, and its cooks, like those in other parts of Italy, depend on the quality of the ingredients rather than elaborate techniques. Then, once the dish is done, it may be worthy of presentation in a great and frivolous display of Venetian glass, lace, silver, and linen.

The vision of Remi, an expanding, almost doge-like culinary empire based in New York, with outposts in Santa Monica, Mexico City, Tel Aviv, and eventually elsewhere, is to understand the past, reflect the present, and without compromising the integrity of what Venice and its food represent, evolve into the future.

The restaurant, a realization of the combined efforts of Adam D. Tihany, the brilliant designer whose Venetian sensibility led to its conception, and Francesco Antonucci, its chef, co-owner, and one of Venice's most outspoken culinary ambassadors, is named for the gondolier's oar. Like the

Figurines inspired by Carnevale, the pre-Lenten festival

oar it is sleek, stylish, and traditional yet finely crafted to cut the water and stay ahead of the next wave.

"I think it's very important to keep the typical, symbolic dishes of Venice alive, and to make sure they do not become phony or watered down," says Antonucci. "But at the same time, I think we can use these dishes as the basis for a contemporary cooking that draws on ideas from all over the Mediterranean and that responds to the new, more sophisticated American and international taste."

Venice, described by the food writer Waverley Root as "a stage setting for an extravaganza," is on Antonucci's mind as he cooks and thinks about food. He brings his heritage to the market and the kitchen.

As for Tihany, he dreams of Venice, the city he has evoked in Remi—New York, a narrow, curving canal of a space fitted with bridging arches, a colorful facade-like mural, glittering Murano chandeliers, and snappy maritime stripes. He would take to heart the words of Henry III of France upon his first visit to Venice: "If I were not the king of France, I would choose to be a citizen of Venice."

Under the arcades of the Rialto market

ESSENTIALS IN THE V·E·N·E·T·I·A·N K·I·T·C·H·E·N

*I*magine going to market every day, selecting the most appealing heads of lettuce and bunches of herbs, being tempted by purple-tinged artichokes the size of plums, rosy-hued red mullet not long out of the sea, freshly quarried slabs of Parmesan cheese, and painterly red-speckled beans. The essence of cooking in Venice begins in the market.

Can this old-world culinary sensibility ever be made compatible with a modern, highly mobile society dependent on the automobile and vast megamarkets with immense shopping carts? With all that is microwavable, deep-freezable, shelf stable? By carefully leavening such expediency with local farmers' markets and quality purveyors of fresh food, an acceptable working relationship between two seemingly opposite points of view can be achieved. The adaptation might offer a fine solution: convenience married to quality. But where compromises must be made, convenience, not quality, should be the first to give way.

Venetian cooking is one of immediacy, of just-made risotto served steaming, just-caught fish tossed on the grill or in the pan, and just-picked arugula, tomatoes, or peaches lightly dressed and carried to the table.

The market determines the menu.

In the case of Venice, the market is the Rialto, acknowledged for centuries to be one of the world's most alluring. The Rialto became the commercial hub of the city in the 13th century, when the two sides of the Grand Canal were linked by a wooden bridge, long the only span across the waterway. In 1588 construction of a stone bridge began. Some 6,000 stakes were driven into the mud to support the single arch, which was completed in 1591. (It was completely restored in 1977.)

For centuries banking offices, grain traders, and butchers clustered around the Rialto. Under the ancient arched market porticoes, fishermen and produce vendors sold their wares, and assorted supporting craftsmen like rope-makers and wine vendors gathered around the place where the Grand Canal makes a sharp turn. They continue to do so today. (For a time there were food vendors in St. Mark's Square, but they never competed with the Rialto.)

No other market is like the Rialto. But with a demanding attitude to inform choices, good quality can also be obtained elsewhere. Oddly enough, the Italian shopper does not handle produce to judge whether a pear is ripe or

The market waits in early morning

Fresh produce to be unloaded

an orange heavy. Probing the goods is replaced with trust in the vendor, who knows that a dissatisfied customer will never return. Only the rare American market deserves such confidence, and the shopper who finds one that does should abandon all others. The effort made in securing first-rate ingredients will result in fine food on the table, for ultimately it is the raw materials, not the recipe, that determine the flavor of the dish.

Given a pantry stocked with a selection of basic ingredients, among them rice, cornmeal, spices and seasonings, tins of anchovies and jars of olives, good olive oil and wine vinegar, some dried porcini perhaps, as well as raisins and candied fruit peel, a trip to the market takes care of the rest. The Venetian table is a simple one, ready on a

moment's notice to satisfy with a bit of salad and prosciutto, a simple risotto, some fresh fish quickly fried, and a piece of fruit.

Because Venetian cooking is so market-driven, the chapters in this book are organized according to categories of ingredients. Recipes are cross-referenced in the beginning of each chapter. A number of suggested Venetian menus are given in the last chapter.

Note: In this book *broil* means to cook food in an oven or broiler with the source of heat coming from above the food; *grill* means to cook food on a grill typically not in an oven with the source of the heat coming from below the food, like a barbecue.

Here are some of the basic ingredients, along with guidelines for selection and storage.

Anchovies: Anchovies are imported. Some of the best large and meaty fillets are sold in bulk in Italian fish markets or come canned from the south of Spain.

Artichokes: Tiny artichokes are prized for stewing or sautéing. Refrigerate them and use within a day of purchase.

Arugula: Once a rarity, arugula is now sold year-round. But it is best to look for it when the weather is cool. The leaves will be a deeper green and the flavor will be more intense but less bitter. Rinse and dry arugula well and use it within a day of purchase. Remove heavy stems.

Asiago: A satiny cow's milk cheese from the Veneto, Asiago is becoming increasingly popular elsewhere. Young Asiago has the nutty richness of Cheddar, and when well-aged it is good for grating.

Asparagus: Slender spears of asparagus can be mingled with risotto or pasta; fat ones are excellent for baking. Asparagus are available all year, but the first of the spring season offer special delight.

Clams: In Venice or elsewhere it is essential to purchase clams only from reliable fishmongers whose source of supply is certified beds. The best substitute for Venetian *vongole veraci* are Long Island littlenecks, West Coast Manila clams, or New Zealand cockles. There is no substitute for slender Venetian razor clams. Tiny steamers from Maine come the closest to them in terms of flavor.

Coffee: Like the rest of Italy, Venetians dote on the inky, strong essence of espresso, with its layer of fine beige froth, or *crema*, on top. Use fresh, dark-roasted, finely ground espresso beans.

Cornmeal: For polenta, stone-ground organic cornmeal is preferable. White cornmeal has a finer texture than yellow. Store it in an airtight container.

Cuttlefish (and squid): Cuttlefish (*seppie*)—similar to squid (*calamari*) but with more rounded bodies—are preferred over squid for recipes calling for ink. The cuttlefish has more of it. For frying, tender small squid are better.

Dried beans: The dried bean most often used in Venice is the reddish borlotti bean, not the white Tuscan cannellini. Although dried beans look like they last forever,

Greens and carrots on their way to the kitchen

Vegetables displayed in the market

they are actually better and cook to a more uniformly succulent texture when they are relatively fresh. Some cooks never soak dried beans. But there is no harm in soaking them, and often some good results. Beans need not be soaked more than four hours.

Duck: All manner of duck meat can be used in Venetian recipes, from domestic ducks to the wild variety. Leftover roast duck makes an excellent sauce for pasta.

Fennel: A celery-like vegetable with an anise flavor, fennel can be used in salads, baked with cheese, or cooked until tender, then puréed. Select firm, medium-size bulbs without traces of brown. They will last for several days in the refrigerator.

Figs: Fresh figs, both green and black, are sold in summer and fall. They should be plump, firm but not hard, with no bruises or oozing spots. Keep them refrigerated.

Garlic: Garlic is used with restraint in Venetian cooking. Always buy large, firm, heavy heads. Keep garlic in the skin at room temperature in a covered container that allows air to circulate.

Herbs: Use fresh herbs whenever possible. With either fresh or dried herbs, buy small quantities to use before they wilt or go stale.

Monkfish: Also called *lotte* (its French name), monkfish is actually just the tail of a large, ugly scavenger. Most fish markets sell monkfish tails of varying size without the central bone. Small monkfish tails with bone can be extremely succulent.

Mushrooms: An astonishing variety of wild and cultivated mushrooms is now available, including shiitake, portobello, cremini, chanterelles, oyster mushrooms, and morels, as well as common white mushrooms. It is best not to store fresh mushrooms airtight in plastic. They will rot. Keep them open to the air in a basket or a plain paper bag. A bit of drying will not damage them and, in the case of plain white mushrooms, will intensify and improve the flavor.

Mussels: Cultivated mussels can be excellent. But whenever possible, look for mussels that are smaller rather than very large.

Nuts: Walnuts, hazelnuts (filberts), almonds, and pignoli are frequently used in Venetian cooking. Nuts keep best in the freezer and are improved by lightly toasting before use.

Olive oil: Extra virgin olive oil that is not overly aggressive and herbaceous is imported from Liguria and Apulia. Some also comes from Tuscany, Spain, and even California. Store olive oil in a dark container away from heat.

Olives: Venetian cooking calls for green, not black, olives. But good imported black olives (not the California "ripe" variety) can be used in some recipes and for snacking.

Onions: As important in Venetian cooking as in other cuisines, onions, stored at room temperature, should always be kept on hand in an assortment of sizes.

Parmesan cheese: Use only genuine Parmigiano-Reggiano imported from Italy. Buy smaller rather than larger quantities so it does not dry out excessively. Grate or shave it only as needed. And, contrary to popular advice, never try to freeze it. The only substitute is Grana Padano, a similar cheese made near Parma.

Pasta: Good-quality dried pasta is an important kitchen staple. Keep spaghetti, linguine, and penne on hand. Thick whole wheat spaghetti called bigoli is frequently used in Venice. Italian imports from Abruzzi are among the best commercial pasta.

Peaches: Whether yellow or white, peaches are best in midsummer, to be used within a day or so of purchase.

Peas: June and July are the months when fresh garden peas are at their best.

Peppers: Sweet red or yellow peppers (capsicums) will keep in the refrigerator for several days. They are often seared over a flame, then peeled before using. Good roasted peppers are also available in jars or sold in fancy food shops.

Potatoes: Idaho baking potatoes are the best for recipes like gnocchi and mashed potatoes calling for a dry, fluffy texture.

Prosciutto: Cured Italian prosciutto from Parma is the sweetest and best to use for most purposes.

Pumpkin: Italian pumpkin, a type of squash, tends

Venetian pumpkins

to be less watery and more intensely flavored than American pumpkins. Look for calabaza, a West Indian squash, as a good substitute, or use butternut squash.

Radicchio: There are several varieties of this typically Venetian vegetable related to endive. The kind from Chioggia, now the most common, is mainly purple with white streaks and forms rounded heads, like small cabbages. Radicchio from Treviso is elongated, with loose bunches of whitish leaves edged in red. Radicchio from Castelfranco has more rounded leaves, a pinker color, and a somewhat more bitter flavor.

Raisins: Buy large, good-quality golden and black raisins, preferably organic. Store them airtight.

Rice: Pearly, plump Italian superfino rices (arborio, vialone nano, and carnaroli) are the only varieties of rice to use for risotto. Venetians tend to prefer the slightly smaller-grained vialone nano.

Francesco Antonucci and Adam D. Tihany in the market with Pina Pinella, a vendor of pumpkins.

Salt: Kosher or sea salt is preferred.

Sardines: Fresh sardines are not easy to find, but when they are in the market, buy them for grilling or roasting.

Spices: When purchasing spices, buy small quantities and replace them frequently. Spices should be stored away from heat and light, preferably in opaque containers.

Tomatoes: There is no substitute for exceptionally fresh, vine-ripened tomatoes. When they are out of season, it is best to use good-quality canned tomatoes of the San Marzano variety imported from Italy. Ripe plum or round tomatoes can be roasted and then stored in the freezer for later use.

Vinegar: Good-quality white and red wine vinegars are best for Venetian cooking. Balsamic vinegar, a specialty of Modena in the neighboring region of Emilia-Romagna,

Watermelons for summer

Ripe tomatoes and eggplant

does not figure in Venetian cooking, but some chefs are starting to use it. Fine-quality balsamic vinegar to use sparingly is expensive but worth the investment. Cheap commercial balsamic vinegar is sweet and acrid, and should not be used.

Watermelon: Look for small watermelons in season. The most typical Venetian dessert in summer is slices of watermelon.

Zucchini: Essentially a summer vegetable, zucchini (courgettes) should be purchased unbruised, dark green, slender, and about 6 inches (15 cm) long. Use zucchini within a day of purchase.

Tuna Carpaccio, recipe on page 45

A·N·T·I·P·A·S·T·O

Ornamenting the fabric of Venetian life are the cafés and wine bars dotting the narrow streets and campos, or squares. At varying times of day, the Venetian may stop for a coffee or a glass of wine and a snack.

In the 17th century the Venetian snacked on a kind of sweet bread called *ciambolinin,* accompanied by glasses of sweet wine. Today's taste is for a glass of white wine called *ombra* (see page 165) and cicchetti, tidbits that may consist of a few olives or a piece of cheese or may be more elaborate.

Once at table, the Venetian, like other Italians, begins with a dish or dishes that, while light, are invariably somewhat piquant, designed to whet the appetite. Grilled or boiled seafood splashed with lemon, a tangle of salad greens dressed with sweet-and-sour vegetables are typical.

Some of the antipasti recipes in this chapter are suitable as hors d'oeuvres for snacking. Francesco's addictive crisped potato slices or his tangy green olives crusted with bread crumbs belong in this category.

More substantial, to serve before the risotto, polenta, or pasta course, are plates of beef or tuna carpaccio, salads with anchovies or fava beans, stuffed zucchini (courgette) flowers, or a hearty country terrine.

When necessary, a well-stocked pantry can substitute for actual preparation. Good-quality tinned anchovies, roasted red peppers (capsicums), olives, Parmesan cheese, grissini, and, although they are not Venetian, some sundried tomatoes will go a long way toward assembling a plate of antipasti. Just add good bread.

In other chapters in this book there are more recipes suitable for serving as an antipasto course:

VEGETABLES
Carrot Soup with Prosecco, page 91
Fennel Soup with Lobster, page 92
Cauliflower Soup, page 93
Artichokes in Herb Sauce, page 95
Roasted Shiitake Mushrooms, page 96
Melanzane Funghetto, page 99
Stuffed Zucchini, page 102

SEAFOOD
Fried Calamari, page 118
Shrimp with Artichokes, page 119
Sea Scallops with Bean Cream, page 120

POULTRY, MEAT & GAME
Chicken Stuffed with Prosciutto and Fontina, page 126
Tongue with Olive Sauce, page 133

SAGE POTATO CHIPS

*T*he snack served at Remi's bar is not the typical cicchetti snack—a bit of cheese or sausage—that the visitor to Venice might find in one of that city's wine bars to accompany the ombra, or glass of white wine. Remi's appetite-whetting specialty is a carefully wrought potato chip made of two parchment-thin slices of potato sandwiching a sage leaf. These chips, brushed with clarified butter and browned in the oven, are child's play to construct. And kept in a tightly closed container, they last several days—that is, if no one knows they're available.

"Lots of places serve pieces of focaccia at the bar these days," says Francesco. But just as he is convinced that Venetians make the best risotto, he concedes that "to do a good focaccia you have to come from Genoa." So he makes these irresistible potato chips instead. For festive occasions he substitutes thin slices of black truffle for the sage. One bit of advice: do not wash the potatoes after they have been peeled or put the slices in water. "You don't want to remove the starch," Francesco cautions.

Preheat the oven to 350°F (180°C). Line a large baking sheet with parchment paper, and brush the paper with some of the butter.

Using a mandoline or an electric slicer, slice the potatoes lengthwise very thin. Keep the slices in order, as if you were going to reconstruct the potatoes.

Starting from the side of a potato, place 2 adjacent slices together with a sage leaf sandwiched in between. As the pairs of potato slices are assembled, place them close to each other but not overlapping on the baking sheet. Brush them lightly with butter.

Place in the oven and bake 15 to 20 minutes, turning them once as the edges brown. Remove from the oven and allow them to cool on racks. Serve or store in an airtight container.

MAKES 24 LARGE "CHIPS," 4 TO 6 SERVINGS.

INGREDIENTS

¼ cup (60 g) clarified butter

2 baking potatoes, peeled

24 fresh sage leaves

SALVIA ALLA MILANESE

INGREDIENTS

48 fresh sage leaves

⅓ cup (45 g) flour

1 large egg yolk, lightly beaten

½ cup (60 g) fine dry bread crumbs

6 tablespoons (90 g) clarified butter

Salt to taste

*F*rancesco says that sage prepared this way can be used as a garnish for pastas, fish, meat, or vegetables. And there's nothing wrong with just nibbling it as a snack.

Dip the sage leaves into the flour, then into the egg yolk, then into the bread crumbs.

Heat the butter in a skillet. Brown the sage leaves lightly on each side, then set on absorbent paper to drain. Dust lightly with salt and serve at once or set aside and warm in a 250°F (120°C) oven before serving.

MAKES 8 TO 10 SERVINGS.

CICCHETTI OLIVES

INGREDIENTS

36 pitted green olives

¼ cup (30 g) flour

1 large egg, beaten

⅓ cup (45 g) fine dry bread crumbs

Vegetable oil for deep frying

Venetian bar snacks called cicchetti are similar to tapas. Tapas? In Venice? But consider that Spain was a destination of Venice's far-flung merchants. Furthermore, given the theory that the custom of tapas might have been of Moslem origin and that the Arabs were also trading partners of Venice, it is hardly surprising that such snacks are now commonplace in the city.

These savories might well include the sage potato chips served at Remi, but traditionally they amount to simpler fare. Fried green olives are among the more intriguing and irresistible examples. It should be noted that in the region around Venice the olives served are invariably green. They come from the Lago di Garda. "Black olives are from the south of Italy," explains Francesco.

In addition to this and the following recipe, some other classic cicchetti include hard-cooked eggs sliced in half and topped with an anchovy, a plate of small grilled sardines, pieces of grilled sausage, and nuggets of cheese. Whatever the case, "they must be eaten with the fingers," Francesco insists.

Place the olives in a bowl, cover with cold water, and allow them to soak at least 15 minutes, to remove some of the salt. Rinse the olives and dry them well.

Toss the olives lightly in the flour, then dip each in beaten egg. Roll them in the bread crumbs to coat, place on a plate, and refrigerate one hour.

Heat enough oil for deep frying in a skillet. Place the olives in the oil and fry them, rolling them around to brown them evenly, until they are golden. Drain on absorbent paper and serve while still warm. They can be held for a few hours, then reheated in a 250°F (120°C) oven.

MAKES 6 TO 8 SERVINGS.

CICCHETTI POLENTA WITH ONIONS AND SAUSAGE

*F*or these cicchetti the slice of polenta doubles as a cracker, much the way slabs of it replace bread in the mountains of the Alto Adige. The sausage, luganega, is a spicy specialty of Belluna, in the mountains. In Venice proper a piece of grilled sardine, a grilled shrimp, or a morsel of meat or fried fish from dinner the day before might top the polenta. "You find that leftovers make fine cicchetti," Francesco says.

INGREDIENTS

2 cups (500 ml) water

½ cup (90 g) yellow cornmeal for polenta

Salt to taste

1½ tablespoons extra virgin olive oil

1 onion, sliced thin

1 bay leaf

8 ounces (250 g) luganega sausage or
   12 medium-size shrimp (prawns), shelled

Sprigs of flat-leaf (Italian) parsley

Bring the water to a simmer in a small saucepan. Gradually stir in the cornmeal and cook, stirring, about 15 minutes, until the mixture has thickened. Season with salt and stir in 1 tablespoon of the olive oil.

Spread the cornmeal mixture to a thickness of ½ inch (1.3 cm) on a baking sheet and allow to cool.

Heat the remaining oil in a medium-size nonstick skillet. Add the onion and the bay leaf and cook over medium-low heat about 10 minutes, until the onion turns light gold. Stir in 2 tablespoons (30 ml) water, remove the bay leaf, and remove the skillet from the heat.

Grill the sausage until browned and cooked through. (If using shrimp, toss them with ½ tablespoon olive oil and grill them or sear briefly in a nonstick pan.)

To serve, cut the polenta into 2-inch (5-cm) circles with a glass or a biscuit cutter. Heat a grill, a nonstick skillet, or a griddle, and grill the polenta circles until they are warmed and lightly browned. Top each with some of the onion and a parsley leaf. Cut the sausage on a sharp diagonal into slices about ½ inch (1.3 cm) thick and place on top or, if desired, substitute the shrimp.

MAKES ABOUT 12 PIECES, OR 4 TO 6 SERVINGS.

ROSEMARY GRISSINI

INGREDIENTS

1½ cups (375 ml) warm water

1 cake fresh yeast

Pinch of sugar

2 tablespoons (30 ml) extra virgin olive oil, plus about ⅓ cup for oiling bowl, pans, and dough

1 tablespoon salt

5 cups (670 g) flour (approximately)

2 tablespoons minced fresh rosemary leaves

1 teaspoon minced fresh oregano leaves

Freshly ground black pepper to taste

The grissini (bread sticks) served at Remi are positively addictive. Not only are they excellent to serve with meals, but they are superb to have on hand as a snack with drinks. The restaurant makes reams of them daily, cutting the dough not by hand but with the wide fettuccine cutter of the pasta machine. "When we discovered the pasta machine, it was such a time-saver," declares Francesco. It's a trick he picked up from another chef who was nearly fired when the owner of the restaurant found out he was not making the grissini by hand! "We don't have such a tough attitude here," Francesco says.

Place ½ cup (125 ml) of the water in a bowl, stir in the yeast and sugar, and set aside to proof for 10 minutes.

Add the remaining water, 2 tablespoons (30 ml) of the oil, and the salt. Begin stirring in the flour, and when it forms a dough, turn it out onto a floured board and knead it for about 10 minutes, kneading in enough of the remaining flour so the dough is fairly firm, dry, and not at all sticky. Knead in the rosemary, oregano, and pepper.

Oil a large bowl, place the dough in the bowl, cover it lightly, and set it in the refrigerator to rise until doubled in bulk, about 6 hours.

Punch the dough down, divide it in quarters, and pinch off egg-sized pieces. Roll each piece to less than ½ inch (1.3 cm) thick. Cut into very narrow strips, each about 12 inches (30 cm) long. Alternatively, you can cut the dough by running it through the widest noodle-cutter setting on a pasta machine.

Oil baking sheets and place the strips of dough about an inch (2.5 cm) apart on the sheets. Brush the strips lightly with oil and set them aside to rise for 1 hour.

Preheat the oven to 375°F (190°C). Place the sheets in the oven and bake until the bread sticks are uniformly golden brown, about 20 minutes. Allow them to cool on racks before serving. Store them in an airtight container once they have cooled completely.

MAKES ABOUT 100 BREAD STICKS.

INGREDIENTS

1 envelope (¼ ounce/7 g) active dry yeast

1 cup (250 ml) warm water

1 teaspoon salt

5 tablespoons (75 ml) extra virgin olive oil,
    plus extra for coating bowl

½ teaspoon coarsely ground black pepper

2 teaspoons chopped fresh rosemary leaves

3 to 3½ cups (375 to 435 g) flour

1 large onion, chopped

4 roasted tomatoes (8 if they are plum
    tomatoes) (recipe on page 71), or 8 well-
    drained canned plum (egg) tomatoes

16 large canned flat anchovy fillets

VENETIAN PIZZA

*T*hese individual pizzas are delicious eaten as a snack, cut into wedges to make an hors d'oeuvre, or served with a salad for lunch or supper. Since pizza is not traditionally Venetian, what gives this pizza its Venetian character? Francesco has a simple answer: "Onions. The minute you put onions on, it becomes Venetian." The anchovy reinforces the pizza's Venetian flavor. As with so many other dishes, Francesco has strong opinions about making pizza. "The problem with a lot of pizza is that the tomato is overcooked," he says. "The tomato cooks on the pizza, so it does not need much cooking before."

Dissolve the yeast in ¼ cup (60 ml) of the water in a large bowl and set aside to proof about 10 minutes. Stir in the remaining water, the salt, 3 tablespoons (45 ml) of the oil, the pepper, and the rosemary. Stir in about half the flour, until the mixture forms a soft dough that leaves the sides of the bowl.

Turn the dough out on a floured board and knead about 8 minutes, kneading in additional flour until the dough is elastic and no longer sticky. Place the ball of dough in a clean oiled bowl. Turn the dough to oil on all sides, cover, and set aside to rise until doubled, 3 to 4 hours in the refrigerator or about 1 hour at room temperature. Punch the dough down.

While the dough is rising, heat the remaining 2 tablespoons (30 ml) oil in a skillet. Add the onion and cook very slowly, stirring, for about 20 minutes, until the onion is tender and has turned a deep gold. Add 2 tablespoons (30 ml) cold water to stop the cooking and remove from the heat.

Preheat the oven to 450°F (230°C). Line a baking sheet with parchment paper.

Divide the dough into 4 portions and shape each into a round about 7 inches (18 cm) in diameter. Make the rounds a little thinner around the edges than in the middle. Spread the onion on each round. Coarsely chop the tomatoes and scatter them on the onion, then top with 4 anchovy fillets. Place on the baking sheet.

Place in the oven on the lowest rack and bake 15 to 20 minutes, until the dough is lightly browned.

MAKES 4 SMALL PIZZAS.

Venetian Pizza

INGREDIENTS

1 cup (125 g) freshly grated Parmesan cheese

PARMESAN SHELL

It takes a good nonstick skillet—hardly a traditional Venetian utensil—to make a crisp, delicate shell of Parmesan cheese. The shell can be filled with arugula salad, grilled or sautéed mushrooms, or even risotto. "It's sometimes crazy the things chefs think up, but that's what makes our business fun," Francesco says. For this and all the other recipes calling for Parmesan cheese, it is essential to use genuine Parmigiano-Reggiano imported from Italy. The name is stamped on the rind. The only possible substitute is Grana Padano imported from Italy, a cheese from the neighboring district. The following recipe makes four medium-size shells.

Place a 7-inch (18-cm) nonstick skillet over medium heat. Have a small bowl, 4 to 5 inches (10 to 13 cm) in diameter, ready on the counter. Turn the bowl upside down.

When the pan is moderately hot, pour ¼ cup (30 g) of the cheese into the pan and quickly tip the pan to coat the bottom, as if making a crepe. Shake out any excess. Cook briefly until any little white bubbles have disappeared and the cheese begins to color around the edges. Carefully lift up the layer of Parmesan and turn it over. Cook it for a few seconds longer, then lift it out and place it briefly on the small overturned bowl to form it into a shell. Allow to cool a minute or so, then gently lift it off.

Repeat with the remaining cheese to make 3 more shells. Set aside at room temperature up to 2 hours, until ready to serve. The crisped cheese can also be cooled flat, then broken into large pieces to serve as a snack.

MAKES 4 SERVINGS.

GOAT CHEESE WITH TOMATO SAUCE

Like those irresistible grissini, a dish of silken, warmed goat cheese paired with a subtly rough-edged tomato sauce entices diners as they are seated at Remi. "It's something to put in the mouth that does not spoil the appetite," says Francesco. In preparing this dish, he points out that basil leaves should not be cut with a knife because that will cause them to blacken. "You have to tear them."

In order to retain the balance of cheese and warm sauce, Francesco does not recommend serving one large mound of cheese surrounded by sauce for a large party. "Keep the portions small and place a dish between each two guests at the table so they can share," he says. "That will give people a chance to be friendly." For a smaller group half the amount of the cheese recipe can be made. Extra tomato sauce can be frozen.

Mash the goat cheese and cream cheese together with a wooden spoon. Work in the mashed roasted garlic, torn basil, and thyme. Stir in 4 tablespoons (60 ml) of the olive oil. Refrigerate this mixture at least 1 hour.

Heat the remaining tablespoon (15 ml) of oil in a medium-size skillet. Add the onion and minced garlic and sauté over medium heat until they are tender but not brown. Stir in the tomatoes, breaking them up with a fork. Cook, uncovered, over very low heat about 40 minutes, until the sauce is smooth. Season with salt and pepper and add the pinch of sugar. Remove from the heat and transfer to a bowl. Place the whole basil leaves on top. Set aside or refrigerate until ready to serve.

Before serving, bring the tomato sauce to a simmer.

To serve, place about ¼ cup (60 g) of the cheese mixture in a mound on each of 6 small, shallow dishes. Spoon about ⅓ cup (80 ml) of the warm tomato sauce around the cheese and serve.

MAKES ABOUT 12 SERVINGS.

INGREDIENTS

4 ounces (125 g) Montrachet or other fresh goat cheese

4 ounces (125 g) cream cheese

5 cloves roasted garlic, mashed (recipe on page 71)

6 fresh basil leaves, torn in tiny pieces

I teaspoon fresh thyme leaves

5 tablespoons (75 ml) extra virgin olive oil

I onion, finely chopped

I clove garlic, minced

I 28-ounce (875 g) can plum (egg) tomatoes

Salt and freshly ground black pepper to taste

Pinch of sugar

4 whole fresh basil leaves

WATERCRESS, FAVA BEAN, AND PECORINO SALAD

INGREDIENTS

I large bunch watercress

12 ounces (375 g) whole fresh fava (broad) beans

¼ cup (30 g) golden raisins

6 tablespoons (90 ml) fruity extra virgin olive oil

4 ounces (125 g) pecorino cheese, in thin shavings

Salt and freshly ground black pepper to taste

What makes a chef? It might be the meticulous care with which an expert like Francesco automatically attends to certain tasks in a manner that few home cooks routinely match. Before he uses watercress for a salad, he takes the time to pick off the leaves like a florist so there will be no stems in the way. He uses the same tactic with the fresh herbs that go into so much of his food, again carefully pulling off the leaves. Once these techniques become habit, it's impossible to handle food otherwise. Call it pride of workmanship, but it's also what makes for fine cooking. This is a fresh, stylish salad.

Pick the leaves off the stems of the watercress and discard the stems.

Remove the fava beans from the long pods, place them in a saucepan, cover with water, and simmer 3 minutes. Drain and transfer the beans to a bowl of ice water.

Place the raisins in a dish of warm water and set aside to soak for 15 minutes.

Peel the skins off the fava beans. Drain the raisins and pat them dry.

Arrange the watercress leaves on each of 4 plates. Scatter the fava beans and raisins over the watercress, drizzle with the olive oil, then top with shavings of pecorino. Season with salt and pepper and serve.

MAKES 4 SERVINGS.

INGREDIENTS

¼ cup (30 g) walnut halves

2 bunches arugula (rocket), rinsed, dried, and heavy stems removed

¾ cup (180 ml) walnut-olive vinaigrette (recipe below)

I ounce (30 g) Parmesan cheese, in thin shavings

12 to 16 sweet-and-sour shallots (recipe on page 39) (optional)

INGREDIENTS

¼ cup (30 g) pitted Kalamata olives

3½ tablespoons (25 g) coarsely chopped walnuts

½ cup (125 ml) red wine vinegar

I½ cups (375 ml) extra virgin olive oil

Freshly ground black pepper to taste

ARUGULA SALAD WITH PARMESAN CHEESE AND WALNUT-OLIVE DRESSING

*F*rancesco devised this salad—"one of the most popular salads we serve at Remi"—as a medley of flavors. The bitterness of the arugula is contrasted by the slightly salty dressing and the nutty cheese. The shallots, if they are added, provide a classically Venetian balance of sweetness. The result is a dish of unusual character, having all four main flavor groups—sweet, sour, salty, and bitter. That might account for the salad's uncommon appeal. It is important to rinse and dry arugula very thoroughly. Removing the heavy stems makes it more attractive to serve.

Toast the walnuts in a toaster oven or by tossing them in a dry skillet over medium heat.

Place the arugula in a large bowl and toss with the vinaigrette dressing.

Divide the arugula among 4 plates. Top each portion with some shaved Parmesan and a scattering of walnuts. Garnish each plate, if desired, with 3 to 4 sweet-and-sour shallots.

MAKES 4 SERVINGS.

WALNUT-OLIVE DRESSING

"*T*his is my invention." Francesco says he was inspired one day when he heard a chef talking about an olive dressing. The addition of walnuts helps mellow the intensity of the olives. A more typically Venetian rendition would require green olives, but Kalamata olives, with their lovely mellow flavor, are better suited to the dressing.

Combine the olives and walnuts in a food processor and chop them together to make a fine mixture, nearly a paste.

Add the vinegar and process briefly. Then, with the machine running, add the oil through the feed tube.

Season the dressing with pepper.

MAKES 2 CUPS.

SWEET-AND-SOUR SHALLOTS

"*Sweet-and-sour is a typically Venetian flavor. Fish, vegetables, meats, game, and even fruits are done this way.*" *Francesco's taste for sweet-and-sour is truly Venetian. The preservative properties of both sugar and acid have long been recognized. In Venice the two are combined, often in a savory mix of onions, pine nuts, and raisins glazed with vinegar, a preparation called "in saor." Adam Tihany has always been intrigued by the taste for sweet-and-sour dishes in both Venetian and Chinese cooking. He likes to think of it as a legacy of Marco Polo, the quintessential culinary manifestation of the meeting of the two cultures.*

At Remi, Francesco's staff prepares tender, well-glazed sweet-and-sour shallots each day to use as garnishes, not only for salads but also for fish, meats, and vegetables, to add a mellow yet piquant suggestion of "in saor" to many dishes.

INGREDIENTS

24 shallots, peeled

1½ cups (375 ml) vegetable stock (recipe on page 85)

2 tablespoons (30 ml) extra virgin olive oil

1½ teaspoons sugar

6 tablespoons (90 ml) red wine vinegar

Place the shallots in a saucepan, add the stock, and simmer gently 25 to 30 minutes, until the shallots are tender. Much of the stock will evaporate.

Heat the oil in a skillet and stir in the sugar. Add the shallots along with any remaining stock and cook over medium heat until the shallots become brown and glazed. Stir in the vinegar and cook a few minutes longer, so the shallots are just coated with a syrupy sweet-and-sour sauce. Store in the refrigerator until ready to use.

MAKES 4 SERVINGS AS A GARNISH.

ENDIVES WITH WHITEBAIT

INGREDIENTS

1 large egg yolk

1½ teaspoons white wine vinegar

¼ cup (60 g) Dijon mustard

4 canned anchovy fillets, mashed

⅔ cup (160 ml) vegetable oil

2 tablespoons (30 ml) water

3 whole Belgian endives (witloof/chicory),
　　cores removed

12 imported *alici* (whitebait) cured in vinegar

1½ teaspoons minced fresh chives

In describing Renaissance dinners in Venice, visitors marveled at the table settings—glass-ware and forks, items unheard of in other cities—and the luxury of the repasts. Among the dishes preceding the meat were bottarghe *(mullet roe),* alici *(whitebait),* capperi *(capers),* olive *(olives), and* caviale *(caviar), along with salads made with lime juice and preserved flowers.*

At Remi an appetizer of alici *marinated in vinegar is combined with snowy, slightly bitter endive and mellowed with a rich mayonnaise. Francesco advises that if you cannot obtain cured* alici, *omit them. But if the radicchio of Treviso, with its long leaves, is available, it can be used in place of the endives. As for making homemade mayonnaise, it's a simple task. "And if you do not know how to make it, the mustard will help hold it together," says Francesco. He adds that the Venetians sometimes use a little mashed potato to stabilize it. Regardless, be sure to use an egg from a reliable source to avoid any possibility of contamination. If necessary, ½ cup (125 g) commercial mayonnaise can be substituted for the mixture of egg yolk, oil, and vinegar.*

Place the egg yolk in a food processor, add the vinegar, mustard, and mashed anchovies, and process the mixture until smooth. Alternatively, place the egg yolk in a bowl and whisk in the other ingredients. With the machine running, slowly add the oil through the feed tube and process the mixture until it is thick. Or beat the oil in slowly by hand. Beat in the water to thin the mixture slightly.

Spoon about 3 tablespoons (45 ml) of the sauce on each of 4 plates.

Sliver the endives lengthwise and spread the slivers over the sauce on the plates. Top with the *alici* and sprinkle with chives.

MAKES 4 SERVINGS.

INGREDIENTS

5 cups (1.25 l) water

2 cups (500 ml) white vinegar

¼ cup (60 g) sugar

1 tablespoon salt

1 tablespoon black peppercorns

1½ teaspoons juniper berries

8 heads radicchio

2 cups (500 ml) extra virgin olive oil

½ bunch flat-leaf (Italian) parsley

Marinated radicchio

MARINATED RADICCHIO

"*I* learned this recipe from my friends at Ristorante Celeste in Treviso," Francesco says. "It's so beautiful." Marinating the radicchio removes some of the bitterness from the vegetable and also intensifies the color. In Treviso they serve it with salami, but Francesco prefers it with prosciutto or octopus.

Bring the water, vinegar, sugar, salt, 2 teaspoons black peppercorns, and 1 teaspoon juniper berries to a boil in a large, deep saucepan.

If using round heads of radicchio, quarter them. Bunches of long Treviso radicchio can be left whole. Place the radicchio in the saucepan and cook for 6 to 7 minutes, then drain it well.

Transfer the radicchio to a bowl or a large jar and cover it with the oil. Add the remaining peppercorns and juniper berries and tuck in the parsley. Cover and marinate the radicchio for 4 to 5 hours before using. It will keep for a week.

Makes 12 to 16 servings.

MARINATED RADICCHIO AND OCTOPUS SALAD

C ombining the marinated radicchio with the octopus results in a handsome dish with a rich purple to burgundy color. The succulence and mild sweetness of the octopus complement the tangy and delicately bitter flavor of the radicchio. "The color of the radicchio reminded me of the octopus, which is why I put them together," Francesco explains. As for cooking the octopus, Francesco turns traditional. He throws a few used wine corks into the pot, a technique that is supposed to keep the octopus tender. They say it also works with stew meat. Putting the octopus in cold water after it is boiled helps set the color.

INGREDIENTS

I pound (500 g) cleaned fresh octopus

I cup (250 ml) white vinegar

I tablespoon black peppercorns

2 stalks celery

I onion, quartered

5 cups (1.25 l) water

3 tablespoons (45 ml) extra virgin olive oil

1½ teaspoons red wine vinegar

Salt and freshly ground black pepper to taste

I tablespoon chopped flat-leaf (Italian) parsley

2 to 3 heads marinated radicchio (recipe on page 42), halved

Place the octopus in a deep saucepan with the white vinegar, pepper-corns, celery, onion, and water. There should be enough water to cover the octopus. Add 2 or 3 wine corks. Bring to a simmer and cook for 1 hour.

Drain the octopus and transfer it to a bowl of ice water. Allow it to cool completely.

Slice the octopus in 1-inch (2.5-cm) pieces. Mix the olive oil, red wine vinegar, salt, pepper, and parsley together and toss with the octopus. Allow to marinate at least 1 hour.

Serve the octopus with marinated radicchio on the side.

MAKES 4 SERVINGS.

INGREDIENTS

48 very small littleneck or Manila clams,
cockles, or medium-size mussels

½ cup (125 ml) extra virgin olive oil

4 cloves garlic

¼ cup (60 ml) dry white wine

2 sprigs fresh rosemary, broken

Juice of ½ lemon

Crusty bread

CLAMS VENETIAN STYLE

*V*enetians have their choice of clams, from the little rounded hard-shell clams called vongole veraci *to the pencil-thin razor clams called* cannelli *that are usually split, brushed with butter, and grilled briefly.* Cannelli *do not travel, however, and are a treat to be enjoyed in Venice. Instead, Francesco offers* vongole veraci *quickly steamed with oil and garlic. "At one time in my life I made so many of these you could have built a house with the shells," he says. "For a Venetian the amount in this recipe would be a half portion." It is important to select the smallest clams and to use a very good, fragrant olive oil. The recipe is equally good with mussels.*

Be sure the clams or mussels are well scrubbed. Mussels should be debearded.

In a large, heavy saucepan, heat the oil. Add the garlic and wine, stir, then add the clams or mussels. Stir, then cover and cook over medium heat until the shells open, about 8 minutes.

Transfer the clams or mussels to 2 warm bowls.

Strain the juices from the pan through a very fine strainer or a strainer lined with a piece of muslin or cheesecloth and pour the juices over the clams or mussels.

Scatter the rosemary over each serving and sprinkle with lemon juice. Serve at once with crusty bread.

MAKES 2 SERVINGS.

Venetian razor clams

INGREDIENTS

1 pound (500 g) fresh tuna, in a single slab about 1½ inches (4 cm) thick

1 teaspoon Dijon mustard

1½ teaspoons cracked black peppercorns

1 tablespoon poppy seeds

2 tablespoons (30 ml) basil oil (recipe on page 87)

Lemon wedges

Shavings of pecorino Romano (optional)

TUNA CARPACCIO

A creation of Giuseppe Cipriani, the founder of Harry's Bar in Venice, carpaccio is classically made with paper-thin slices of raw beef drizzled with ribbons of a thin mayonnaise-style sauce. Today, however, chefs are making carpaccios with other meats like veal and also with fish.

"I like using tuna because it looks like beef," Francesco says. Tuna is very bland, so he rolls it in pepper and sears it before chilling and slicing it to serve. At Remi the tuna is cut into a solid one-pound log, which provides attractive round slices. But because of the amount of waste, this is impractical to do at home, where finding use for the scraps of tuna left from trimming would be a challenge. Fortunately, the recipe works equally well with a thick tuna steak. The tuna is cooked wrapped in foil so the spice coating does not scorch.

When buying tuna look for rich rosy fish that is moist but not wet, with no signs of drying around the edges or cracking on the surface. If you do not have a source for impeccable tuna, try preparing the black peppered beef carpaccio (page 46) in its place.

Trim any dark areas off the tuna. Spread both sides with a thin film of the mustard.

Combine the peppercorns and poppy seeds on a flat plate and press them onto the tuna on both sides. Wrap the coated tuna smoothly in a sheet of foil.

Heat a heavy nonstick pan over medium heat. Place the slab of tuna still wrapped in the foil in the pan and cook it for 1½ minutes on one side. Turn it over and cook it for 1 minute on the other side. Remove it from the pan.

Refrigerate the tuna until 1 hour before serving. Place it in the freezer for 1 hour to make it easier to slice.

To serve, remove the foil, cut the tuna into slices about ¼ inch (6 mm) thick, and arrange them on 4 plates. Drizzle with basil oil and serve garnished with lemon wedges and, if desired, some pecorino cheese.

Photograph on page 24.

MAKES 4 SERVINGS.

1 pound (500 g) center-cut beef tenderloin
(fillet), in a single piece

2 tablespoons cracked black peppercorns

1 tablespoon poppy seeds

Salt to taste

2 bunches arugula (rocket), rinsed, dried, and
stems removed

Tarragon dressing (recipe on page 47)

½ to ⅔ cup (60 to 90 g) shaved Parmesan
cheese

BLACK PEPPERED BEEF CARPACCIO WITH TARRAGON DRESSING

*T*his recipe is essentially the same as the tuna carpaccio. Both are named for a 16th-century Venetian painter. Unlike the classic beef carpaccio, Francesco's version is not served totally raw. Its spice, appropriately enough, is black pepper, a commodity controlled by Venice in the 12th century and so precious that in Europe peppercorns were used as currency. The recipe can also be made with veal. As for the Parmesan cheese, Francesco recommends using a potato peeler to cut thin shavings. "In the restaurant we use the meat slicer," he says, "but that's because we have to do a very large quantity every day."

The beef should be well-trimmed but not tied. Place it on a sheet of foil large enough to enclose it.

Mix the peppercorns, poppy seeds, and salt together and spread them on the foil. Roll the beef in the spices to coat the outside, then wrap the beef tightly in the foil.

Heat a heavy nonstick skillet. Place the foil-wrapped beef in the skillet and sear it all around, leaving it to cook about 1 minute on every side, enough to cook the outside but leave the center rare. Remove it from the skillet and refrigerate it for at least 30 minutes.

To serve, unwrap the beef and slice it very thin. Arrange some of the arugula on each plate, then arrange the slices of beef on top. Drizzle each portion with tarragon dressing and top with shavings of cheese.

MAKES 4 TO 6 SERVINGS.

TARRAGON DRESSING

INGREDIENTS

1 large egg yolk

1½ teaspoons Dijon mustard

2 tablespoons (30 ml) fresh lemon juice

1 shallot, very finely minced

1 tablespoon minced fresh tarragon leaves

½ cup (125 ml) corn oil

Salt and freshly ground black pepper to taste

3 tablespoons (45 ml) hot water

Tarragon, an herb now popular in France, is of Arab origin and was introduced to the European table by Crusaders stopping in Venice on their return from Jerusalem. It provides the aromatic grace note for this beef carpaccio with its peppery edge. The dressing calls for a raw egg yolk. It is best to use organic eggs.

Beat the egg yolk with the mustard in a medium-size bowl. Beat in the lemon juice, shallot, and tarragon.

Place the bowl on a pot holder or a folded cloth so it is stable. Then, beating constantly with a whisk, pour in about half the oil in a very thin stream. The mixture should thicken like a mayonnaise. Once about half the oil has been added, beat the mixture for a minute or so until it begins to lighten in color. Then add the remaining oil in a very thin stream, still beating constantly.

When all the oil has been added, continue beating for a few seconds, then season with salt and pepper. Stir in the water.

MAKES 1 CUP
(250 ML).

16 fresh zucchini (courgette) flowers

¾ cup (90 g) flour

3 large eggs

Salt to taste

¼ cup (60 ml) milk

6 ounces (185 g) mozzarella, chopped

3 tablespoons (25 g) drained capers

I oven-dried tomato (recipe on page 71), chopped

I tablespoon chopped fresh basil

Vegetable oil for deep frying

STUFFED ZUCCHINI FLOWERS

Zucchini flowers bespeak Italy in summer. The delicate, pale orange blossoms can encase all manner of lush fillings. Francesco advises using the zucchini flowers the same day you buy or pick them. Also, take care not to brown them too much when frying or the filling will ooze out. He also recommends using commercial mozzarella instead of the best hand-made variety so it will be firmer, less moist.

Gently pull the stamen out of each zucchini flower. Set the flowers aside.

Beat the flour, eggs, and salt together in a bowl until they are smooth. Beat in the milk. Set the batter aside.

Mix the mozzarella, capers, tomato, and basil together and fill the inside of each zucchini flower with some of this mixture. Fold the ends of the petals over the filling to enclose it.

Heat the oil to a depth of 2 inches (5 cm) in a heavy saucepan or a wok.

Dip the stuffed zucchini flowers into the batter, allowing any excess to run off. Fry the zucchini flowers until they turn light gold, 6 to 8 minutes. Drain them on absorbent paper as they are done. Sprinkle them lightly with salt and serve them while they are still warm.

MAKES 4 SERVINGS.

1 pound (500 g) boneless pork neck or shoulder (blade), cubed

4 ounces (125 g) boneless veal neck or shoulder (blade), cubed

8 ounces (250 g) pork fat, cubed

3 tablespoons chopped fresh rosemary leaves

2 tablespoons chopped fresh marjoram leaves

2 teaspoons chopped fresh sage leaves

1 tablespoon crumbled bay leaves

2 tablespoons finely chopped garlic

1 teaspoon juniper berries

1 cup (250 ml) dry white wine

4 ounces (125 g) slab bacon, diced

8 ounces (250 g) cooked beef tongue, finely diced

8 ounces (250 g) boneless smoked pork, finely diced

½ cup (60 g) shelled unsalted pistachio nuts

Kosher salt and freshly ground black pepper

1½ cups (375 g) green sauce (recipe on page 50)

COUNTRY TERRINE

"In the countryside dishes like this are a way to use up odds and ends. It's a dish more from the mountains around Venice than from the city." Francesco's interpretation is rustic and flavorful, and a splendid dish for a party buffet. The herbaceous green sauce provides an elegant counterpoint.

Combine the boneless pork, boneless veal, and pork fat in a large bowl. Add the rosemary, marjoram, sage, bay leaves, garlic, and juniper berries and toss the ingredients together to distribute them evenly. Add the white wine, toss again, cover, and refrigerate 24 hours.

Grind the herbed meats fairly fine in a meat grinder or by pulsing in a food processor.

Cook the bacon in a skillet until it is brown and crisp. Drain it well. Mix it in a bowl with the tongue, smoked pork, and pistachio nuts. Add the ground meats and, using your hands or a large spoon, mix all the ingredients together. Season with pepper and a light sprinkling of coarse salt. Because there is raw pork in the mixture, do not taste it for seasoning. You can make a small mound of it and simmer it for 10 minutes in water in order to taste it to see if it needs more salt.

Preheat the oven to 300°F (150°C). Pack the mixture into a 6-cup (1.5-l) terrine. Place the terrine in a larger baking dish and pour boiling water into the larger dish until it comes halfway up the sides of the terrine. Bake the terrine for 2 hours. Remove the terrine from the oven and place a double thickness of foil on top. Allow it to cool for about 30 minutes.

Using your hands, press down on the top of the meat to compress it and force out excess fat. Weight the top of the terrine with some heavy objects, allow it to cool to room temperature, then refrigerate it, still weighted, overnight.

Remove the terrine from the refrigerator 1 hour before serving with green sauce as an accompaniment.

MAKES 12 SERVINGS.

INGREDIENTS

1 large egg, hard-cooked

⅓ cup (45 g) chopped cornichons (French sour pickles)

1 tablespoon drained capers

⅓ cup (15 g) chopped flat-leaf (Italian) parsley

⅓ cup (45 g) finely ground pistachios or dry bread crumbs

1 tablespoon Dijon mustard

6 tablespoons (90 ml) dry white wine

6 tablespoons (90 ml) extra virgin olive oil

Salt to taste

GREEN SAUCE FOR COUNTRY TERRINE

"*Green sauces are used more in the region around Modena than in Venice, but I like the way they can contrast a rich terrine. This sauce is also good with simply boiled or grilled seafood.*" *Francesco's green sauce is deliciously piquant, an excellent contrast for steamed vegetables or sausages.*

Remove the yolk of the egg and reserve for another use. Chop the white. Combine it with the cornichons, capers, and parsley and chop them very fine. Mix with the pistachios.

Beat the mustard and wine together, then beat in the oil. Combine with the finely chopped pickle mixture. Season with salt. Serve as a condiment with pâtés, boiled meats, chicken, fish, or sausages.

MAKES ABOUT 1½ CUPS (375 G).

PORCINI DUMPLINGS

The Austrian influence on the food of the Alto Adige, the mountainous region north of Venice, is evident in this dish, a typical bread dumpling lightened in texture and enriched in flavor by the addition of porcini mushrooms. It makes a splendid first course served with sautéed or roasted mushrooms (recipe on page 96). "It's for winter," Francesco says. "Slices of it with Parmesan cheese could even be a supper." The earthy, tender dumpling is also excellent served with roast duck, chicken, or veal.

Place the dried porcini in a bowl, cover with warm water, and set aside to soak for 1 hour. Drain the mushrooms, dry them well, and chop them fine.

In a medium-size skillet, heat the oil over medium heat. Add the mushrooms, shallots, garlic, and rosemary and sauté until the shallots are tender and the mushrooms begin to brown.

INGREDIENTS

4 ounces (125 g) dried porcini mushrooms

3 tablespoons (45 ml) extra virgin olive oil

3 tablespoons (25 g) finely chopped shallots

1 clove garlic, crushed

1 tablespoon finely chopped rosemary leaves

2 cups (125 g) crumbled crustless day-old
  white bread

3 tablespoons finely chopped flat-leaf
  (Italian) parsley

3 large eggs

¼ cup (60 ml) milk

Salt and freshly ground black pepper

2 tablespoons (30 g) unsalted butter or
  truffle butter

3 tablespoons (22 g) freshly grated
  Parmesan cheese

Place the bread in a bowl. Remove the garlic clove from the mushroom mixture, add the sautéed mushrooms to the bread, and mix with your hands. Mix in the parsley.

Beat the eggs and milk together and season well with salt and pepper. Mix the egg mixture with the bread and mushroom mixture until well blended. Add more salt and pepper if necessary.

Place the mixture on a clean cotton or linen kitchen towel and form it into a sausage shape about 8 inches (20 cm) long and 2½ inches (6.5 cm) in diameter. Wrap it tightly in the cloth and twist the ends closed. Squeeze any excess liquid out of the roll. Tie the roll in the cloth with string at approximately 2-inch (5-cm) intervals, taking care to tie the ends tightly.

Select a saucepan large enough to hold the roll. Fill it with enough salted water to cover the roll and bring it to a boil. Lower the heat to a simmer, place the roll in the pan, and simmer it for 25 minutes.

Remove the roll from the pan and allow it to drain. Unwrap it and cut it in slices about an inch (2.5 cm) thick. Just before serving, heat the butter in a skillet and lightly brown the slices of dumpling in the butter, turning them once to brown both sides. Serve with Parmesan cheese.

MAKES 6 TO 8 SERVINGS.

POTATO FRITTATA

"I love eggs," says Francesco, but for him an egg dish like this frittata, a simple, rustic, filled omelet, has gone from being an everyday item to something worth a special occasion. "So put some truffle oil on it," Francesco jokes.

INGREDIENTS

2 baking potatoes

8 large eggs

Salt and freshly ground black pepper to taste

⅓ cup (45 g) freshly grated Parmesan cheese

1 tablespoon mixed chopped fresh herbs

2 sun-dried tomatoes, minced

⅓ cup (80 ml) extra virgin olive oil

1 teaspoon truffle oil (optional)

Place the potatoes in a pot with enough water to cover them, bring to a boil, and cook until they are tender, about 40 minutes. Peel them by holding them in a towel, and slice them.

Beat the eggs with the salt and pepper. Stir in the cheese, herbs, and sun-dried tomatoes.

Heat half the olive oil in a 12-inch (30-cm) skillet or use two 8- to 9-inch (20- to 23-cm) skillets. Nonstick skillets will make this recipe easier to prepare. Spread the potato slices in the oil and cook them until they begin to brown, then turn them so the other side browns lightly. Season them with salt and pepper. Be sure none are sticking to the bottom of the pan.

Add the remaining olive oil to the pan or pans, and when it is hot, pour the eggs over the potatoes. Cook over medium heat until the eggs are lightly browned on the bottom. Loosen the eggs around the edges and shake the pan to make sure the frittata is loose in the pan. Flip it over by placing a large plate on the pan, turning both plate and pan over together, then sliding the frittata back into the pan. Cook the frittata another few minutes. Instead of flipping the frittata, the topside of it can be lightly browned under a broiler. Either transfer the frittata to a serving platter or serve it directly from the pan. Drizzle with truffle oil, if desired.

MAKES 3 TO 6 SERVINGS.

EGGS TORTINO

This is the simplest of self-indulgent egg dishes. The recipe is given for one person. Make several tortini and serve them at room temperature for a picnic. A lower-fat version can be made by using 1 whole egg and 2 egg whites instead of 3 whole eggs.

Steam the asparagus about 3 minutes, until they are just tender.

Preheat the oven to 400°F (200°C). Butter a 2-cup (500-ml) shallow baking dish.

Beat the eggs with the milk and add the salt and Parmesan cheese. Pour the mixture into the baking dish and place the asparagus on top. Bake for 15 minutes, then serve.

MAKES 1 SERVING.

INGREDIENTS

4 medium-thick asparagus, peeled

Unsalted butter

3 large eggs

2 tablespoons (30 ml) milk

Pinch of salt

1½ tablespoons freshly grated
    Parmesan cheese

R·I·C·E, P·O·L·E·N·T·A & P·A·S·T·A

A variety of grains bolster the Venetian table. Rice and cornmeal are ubiquitous, like the inevitable pasta.

RICE

Venice's location at the edge of Italy's largest agricultural plain, drained by a vast river system, has given it rice. In a thousand ways, rice is nearly as essential to Venetian cuisine as it is to Chinese. The rice that is cultivated throughout the valley of the Po River and its many tributaries in northern Italy is used mostly for risotto, from the Piedmont in the west to Friuli in the east. But nowhere is risotto as varied, colorful, and glorified as in Venice.

The Italians have the Arabs to thank for rice. They brought rice to Spain in the 9th or 10th century, and the Spanish introduced it to southern Italy. Then in 1475 the duke of Milan gave the duke of Ferrara twelve sacks of rice to plant. Thence began extensive cultivation in the Republic of Venice, and by the next century it was all the rage. *Risi e bisi,* a soupy risotto, is made with the first young peas to celebrate St. Mark's Day, April 25.

Risotto is sometimes tinted with saffron in Venice. Or it may take on the roseate hue of radicchio, a verdant cast from asparagus or a purée of little green lagoon fish called *gò,* or the earthen tones of seasonal wild mushrooms, and frequently it is nearly black from the ink of cuttlefish. Snowy risotto, simply made with butter and Parmesan cheese, is commonplace. Every conceivable vegetable, seafood, and meat can go into risotto. There is even a savory risotto made with grapes. The frugal Venetian does not hesitate to stretch a bit of leftover into half a meal by amplifying it with rice.

Regardless of flavorings, the proper results can be achieved only by using plump, pearly, short to medium grain rice from the Po Valley, the only rice that can be stirred as it cooks without breaking. In Venice risotto is often made with a slightly more liquid consistency than elsewhere in Italy, giving it the surname *all'onda,* "with waves."

Arborio is the most common of the finest, or superfino, risotto rices grown in northern Italy, and the one most widely available elsewhere. Two others, carnaroli and vialone nano, are slightly firmer and sought for risotto by the cognoscenti. Like most Venetians, Francesco prefers vialone nano, which some shops in America and elsewhere now carry.

POLENTA

Porridges called puls or pulmentum had been made from a variety of grains since Roman times, but the Venetians were the first to turn corn from the New World into this staple. In 1861 William Dean Howells, the American consul in Venice, described food shops with "mountains of polenta, plates of minnows, bowls of rice, roast poultry, dishes of snails and liver, and vast heaps of frying fish."

Venetian refinement demanded fine white cornmeal for polenta, and indeed, today white polenta is more common in the city than yellow. Polenta may be the food of the poor, but it takes on an unmistakable elegance in the hands of Venetian cooks.

Outside Venice proper, in the rural, mountainous area of the Veneto, a cauldron-like copper pot of yellow polenta stirred with a long wooden stick offers daily sustenance. Traditionally, the just-cooked steaming mass of cornmeal is turned out on a linen napkin, cut with a length of cotton thread held tight, and served at once. Francesco, who grew up in Mestre, Venice's mainland industrial lifeline, recalls huge platters of polenta enhanced by a sausage or two for dinner. *Polenta e oṣeletti scapai* refers to polenta with the "birds that got away," in other words, served with sausage or mushrooms perhaps, when the hunter came home empty-handed.

Any cornmeal can be used for polenta—an import is unnecessary—but stone-ground cornmeal is best. White cornmeal tends to be finer; yellow usually has a coarser texture. It is simple to make, and leftovers never go to waste.

Freshly made creamy polenta can be as lushly comforting as mashed potatoes. In Venice and elsewhere, it is also permitted to cool thoroughly and transformed on the grill or in the sauté pan into a crisp, gilded cake. Grilled or fried polenta cut into squares can replace bread for an hors d'oeuvre, become the underpinning for sautéed mushrooms,

or complement the strong flavors of country cheese, creamy *baccalà* (salt cod), or spicy cuttlefish in ink.

PASTA

Marco Polo may be the apocryphal father of Italian pasta, but in Venice, where risotto and polenta star, pasta is often of secondary importance. As in other regions of Italy, the type of pasta used in a dish—dry store-bought or freshly made egg pasta—is a function of the flavors and ingredients.

Dry pasta, usually spaghetti, is the type used for most seafood. One exception is ravioli, which is often served with seafood fillings in Venice. Spaghetti is paired with reddish beans for a classic soup, *pasta e fagioli,* or in the soft, sibilant dialect of Venice, "*pasta e fasioi.*"

In this region a kind of thick spaghetti called bigoli made from whole wheat (wholemeal) is served with simple but richly flavored mixtures of anchovies or shreds of duck or game. Gnocchi, the tender little dumplings made of mashed potato and sometimes pumpkin, are another Venetian favorite, also popular in the mountainous area to the north that segues into the Tyrol.

Other dishes using rice, polenta, and grains can be found elsewhere in this book:

ANTIPASTO
Cicchetti Polenta with Onions and Sausage, page 30
Porcini Dumplings, page 50

SWEETS
Polenta Brioche, page 157

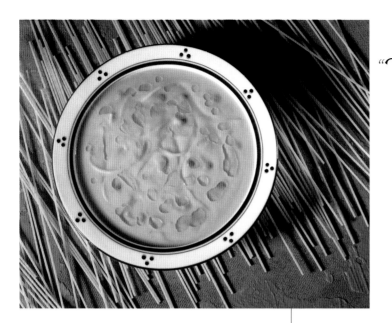

PASTA E FAGIOLI

"*When I was younger and working at my first job at the Hotel Las Vegas near Venice, the chef in charge of the kitchen had me enter a bean soup contest,*" *Francesco recalls.* "*We won it because I used dry pasta, not fresh.*" *Francesco breaks the spaghetti into small pieces by wrapping it first in a napkin, then running the "package" over the edge of a counter. And he finishes the rustic, traditional pasta and bean soup with hot olive oil infused with herbs and garlic.* "*That trick is as old as the pyramids,*" *he says. He also advises preparing the soup the day before it is to be served, for better flavor.*

Place the beans in a bowl, cover with cold water to a depth of I inch (2.5 cm), and allow to soak 4 hours or overnight.

Drain the beans. Heat the bacon and 2 tablespoons (30 ml) of the oil in a heavy 4- to 5-quart (4- to 5-l) saucepan. Add the unpeeled garlic, celery, carrot, onion, and tomato, cook for a few seconds, then add the beans and water. Bring to a simmer and cook, partly covered, for about I hour, until the beans are tender. Skim the surface from time to time.

While the beans are cooking, bring a pot of water to a boil for the spaghetti. Wrap the spaghetti in a cloth towel or napkin and, holding the ends of the cloth closed, run this "package" of spaghetti over the edge of a counter to break the raw spaghetti into small pieces. Drop the spaghetti into the pot of boiling water and cook it about 8 minutes, then drain it and set aside.

When the beans are tender, remove the bacon and the garlic cloves and, using a slotted spoon, remove about half the beans. Purée the remaining bean soup mixture in a blender or a food processor. Add up to a cup of water if the mixture is too thick.

Transfer the puréed soup to a saucepan. Add the cooked spaghetti and reserved beans. Reheat and season with salt and pepper.

Just before serving, heat the remaining olive oil in a skillet and add the crushed garlic cloves and the sprigs of oregano, rosemary, and thyme. Cook for 5 minutes, then strain the hot herb oil into the soup. Serve immediately.

MAKES 4 TO 6 SERVINGS.

INGREDIENTS

1⅓ cups (250 g) dried borlotti (cranberry) beans

2 ounces (60 g) slab bacon, in I piece

½ cup (125 ml) extra virgin olive oil

5 cloves garlic, unpeeled

½ stalk celery, coarsely chopped

I carrot, coarsely chopped

I small onion, coarsely chopped

I plum (egg) tomato

5 cups (1.25 l) water

4 ounces (125 g) dry spaghetti

Salt and freshly ground black pepper

6 cloves garlic, crushed

2 sprigs each fresh oregano, rosemary, and thyme

INGREDIENTS

2 tablespoons (30 ml) extra virgin olive oil

⅔ cup (80 g) chopped onion

2 cups (250 g) fresh shelled peas (about 2½ pounds/1.25 kg peas in the pod)

8 cups (2 l) vegetable stock (recipe on page 85)

¼ cup (60 g) butter

1 cup (150 g) vialone nano or arborio rice

¼ cup (60 ml) dry white wine

Salt and freshly ground black pepper to taste

½ cup (60 g) freshly grated Parmesan cheese

Peas and Rice (Risi e Bisi) *(right),*
Risotto with Asparagus (left)

PEAS AND RICE (RISI E BISI)

Waverley Root, author of The Food of Italy, *wonders whether this simple yet sumptuous creation is a soup or a vegetable dish. Called* risi e bisi *in Venetian dialect, it's more about peas than about rice and is traditionally served on April 25, St. Mark's Day, when the first peas of the region appear in the Rialto market. They are expensive and not as flavorful as the ones that are available a little later. That is why Francesco says the dish is better later in the season, for the feast of the Redeemer, or Redentore, to celebrate the end of the Plague in 1576. Purists insist on peas from Chioggia.*

The texture of the dish is rather soupy, thinner than the typical Venetian risotto all'onda. "It's the only rice dish you can eat with a spoon," Francesco points out. "And the rice cannot be al dente."

Heat the oil in a heavy 3- to 4-quart (3- to 4-l) saucepan. Add the onion and sauté over medium-low heat until it is tender but not brown.

Stir in the peas and 4 cups (1 l) of the stock. Simmer, uncovered, until the peas are very tender, about 30 minutes.

With a slotted spoon, remove half of the peas and reserve. Purée the remaining contents of the saucepan and set aside.

In a clean 3-quart (3-l) saucepan, melt 2 tablespoons (30 g) of the butter. Add the rice and cook over medium heat until it becomes opaque. Stir in the wine, the remaining stock, and the puréed pea mixture.

Simmer gently, stirring from time to time, for 15 minutes. Add half the reserved peas, cook 10 minutes longer, then add the remaining peas and the remaining 2 tablespoons (30 g) of butter. Season with salt and pepper, stir in the Parmesan cheese, and serve in soup plates.

MAKES 6 SERVINGS.

INGREDIENTS

1 pound (500 g) slender asparagus

½ baking potato, peeled and chopped

Salt to taste

3 cups (750 ml) vegetable stock
(approximately) (recipe on page 85)

2 tablespoons (30 ml) extra virgin olive oil

½ cup (60 g) finely chopped onion

1 clove garlic, minced

1½ cups (250 g) vialone nano or arborio rice

½ cup (125 ml) dry white wine

2 tablespoons (30 g) unsalted butter

Freshly grated Parmesan cheese

RISOTTO WITH ASPARAGUS

The plump, pearly, short-grain Italian rice grown in the Po Valley, which can absorb a quantity of liquid and become properly tender without falling apart, is essential for making risotto. Despite what some books say, no other kind of rice will do. "One of the first steps in making risotto is to choose your rice," says Francesco. This risotto is a delicate spring green, to celebrate the first asparagus of the season.

Snap off the ends of the asparagus where they break naturally. Peel the stems if necessary. Cut off the tips and set them aside. Chop the stems.

Place the potato and chopped stems in a saucepan, add 2 cups (500 ml) of water and a pinch of salt, and cook until they are tender, 10 to 15 minutes. Purée the vegetables. Add enough additional water to the purée to make 2 cups (500 ml). Add all but a dozen of the tips to this purée. Place the reserved tips in a saucepan, add 2 cups (500 ml) water and a pinch of salt, bring to a boil, and cook for 2 to 3 minutes. Drain and set aside.

Place the vegetable stock in a saucepan over low heat and start heating it so it barely simmers.

Heat the oil in a heavy saucepan. Add the onion and cook gently until it is translucent. Stir in the garlic. Add the rice and cook, stirring, about 5 minutes. Add the wine, allow nearly all of it to evaporate, then begin adding the mixture of asparagus purée and tips about ¼ at a time, adding more as the liquid in the pan evaporates. When all the purée has been added, continue cooking and stirring the risotto, adding the warm stock a ladleful at a time. Cook, stirring, until the risotto is plump and offers a little resistance to the bite. The risotto should be very moist.

Stir in the butter and serve at once, decorated with the reserved asparagus tips and with Parmesan cheese on the side.

MAKES 4 TO 6 SERVINGS.

RISOTTO WITH WILD MUSHROOMS

INGREDIENTS

10 ounces (315 g) medium-large shiitake
    mushrooms

¼ cup (60 ml) extra virgin olive oil

3 large cloves garlic, sliced

1 teaspoon fresh thyme leaves

4 tablespoons (60 g) unsalted butter

½ cup (60 g) chopped onion

1½ cups (250 g) vialone nano or arborio rice

5 cups (1.25 l) vegetable stock
    (approximately) (recipe on page 85)

⅓ cup (80 ml) dry white wine

Salt and freshly ground black pepper to taste

Freshly grated Parmesan cheese

As an asparagus risotto suggests spring, so this mushroom risotto evokes autumn, when fragrant wild mushrooms, the damp earth still clinging to them, are brought by the basketful to market. Today, with the profusion of wild and cultivated exotic mushrooms in American markets (at increasingly reasonable prices) and elsewhere, this once elusively difficult Italian dish need not be reserved for dining out or a special occasion.

If you cannot find fresh exotic mushrooms in your market, plan ahead. Buy plain white mushrooms, place them in a basket, uncovered, on the kitchen counter, and allow them to dry out and darken a bit for three to four days. Their flavor and color will intensify. Francesco advises cooking the mushrooms separately, then adding them to the risotto. "Cooking raw mushrooms in the risotto may give the dish a muddy flavor."

Remove and discard the stems from the mushrooms. Slice the mushrooms.

Heat the oil in a large, heavy skillet, add the mushrooms and garlic, and sauté over high heat about 5 minutes, to sear the mushrooms. Stir in the thyme and remove from the heat.

In a large, heavy saucepan, melt 3 tablespoons (45 g) of the butter. Add the onion and cook over medium-low heat until it is translucent. Stir in the rice. Cook, stirring, about 5 minutes, until the rice is well coated with the butter and begins to whiten.

Have the stock barely simmering in another saucepan.

Add the wine to the rice, stir, then add 2 ladles of the hot stock. Cook 3 minutes. Stir in the mushrooms.

Continue adding stock, a couple of ladles at a time, stirring and adding more as the stock is absorbed by the rice. Regulate the heat so the rice and stock cook at a steady simmer. After about 15 minutes, the rice should have swelled and become somewhat tender but still a bit hard in the middle. Continue adding stock for another few minutes, as needed, until the rice is plump, offers only the slightest resistance to the bite, and there is just enough thickened, creamy, saucelike broth to moisten the rice.

Stir in the remaining tablespoon of butter, season with salt and pepper, and serve with Parmesan cheese on the side.

MAKES 4 TO 6 SERVINGS.

RISOTTO WITH SHRIMP AND RADICCHIO

In Venice risotto is a religion that must be practiced daily, with careful attention paid to ritual. "Venetians insist that you need at least 10 years of experience to make a good risotto, and then be prepared to attend to it for 18 minutes," Francesco says. "You can't make a phone call." Instead of 10 years, take the time to tend the rice carefully, regulate the heat as the liquid is added, and keep stirring. This risotto, with its elegant burgundy color, balances the sweet richness of seafood with the temptingly bitter edge of radicchio. It is one of the glories of Francesco's repertory.

Bring a pot with 2 quarts (2 l) of water to a boil. Add the shrimp, blanch 30 seconds, then drain.

In a large, heavy saucepan, melt 4 tablespoons (60 g) of the butter. Add the onion and cook over medium-low heat until it is translucent. Stir in the rice. Cook, stirring, about 5 minutes, until the rice is well coated with the butter and begins to whiten.

Have the stock barely simmering in another saucepan.

Add the wine to the rice, stir, then add 2 ladles of the hot stock. Cook 3 minutes. Stir in the radicchio.

Continue adding stock, a couple of ladles at a time, stirring and adding more as the stock is absorbed by the rice. Regulate the heat so the rice and stock cook at a steady simmer. After about 15 minutes, the rice should have swelled and become somewhat tender but still a bit hard in the middle. There should still be some stock left at this point.

Add all but 4 of the shrimp. Stir, then continue adding stock for another few minutes, as needed, until the rice is plump, offers only the slightest resistance to the bite, and there is just enough thickened, creamy, saucelike broth to moisten the rice.

Stir in the cognac and remaining butter. Season with salt and pepper, garnish each serving with a shrimp, top with a bit of parsley, and serve at once.

Photograph on page 54.

MAKES 3 TO 4 SERVINGS.

INGREDIENTS

20 large shrimp (prawns), shelled and deveined

6 tablespoons (90 g) unsalted butter

½ cup (60 g) finely chopped onion

1½ cups (250 g) vialone nano or arborio rice

5 cups (1.25 l) hot seafood stock (approximately) (recipe on page 85)

⅓ cup (80 ml) dry white wine

10 to 12 large radicchio leaves, coarsely chopped

1 tablespoon cognac or brandy

Salt and freshly ground black pepper to taste

1 tablespoon finely chopped flat-leaf (Italian) parsley

BLACK RISOTTO

INGREDIENTS

¼ cup (60 ml) extra virgin olive oil

½ cup (60 g) finely chopped onion

1½ cups (250 g) vialone nano or arborio rice

4 cups (1 l) hot vegetable stock
(approximately) (recipe on page 85)

⅓ cup (80 ml) dry white wine

Cuttlefish in ink, made with 12 ounces
(375 g) cuttlefish (use ½ recipe, page 67)

Salt and freshly ground black pepper to taste

*B*lack risotto represents Venice at its most exotic. Pristine rice is turned shadowy and dark with the ink of a strange-looking sea creature. The taste is exotic too—briny-sweet, peppery, and rich. Francesco says that recently some chefs have made risotto with squid and no ink, to keep the rice white, then just drizzled some cuttlefish or squid ink on top before serving. "That way the dish doesn't look like it came out of the crankcase of your car," he quips.

Heat the oil in a large, heavy saucepan. Add the onion and cook over medium-low heat until it is translucent. Stir in the rice. Cook, stirring, about 5 minutes, until the rice is well coated with the oil and begins to whiten.

Have the stock barely simmering in another saucepan.

Add the wine to the rice, stir, then add 2 ladles of the hot stock. Cook 3 minutes. Stir in the cuttlefish mixture.

Continue adding stock, a couple of ladles at a time, stirring and adding more as the stock is absorbed by the rice. Regulate the heat so the rice and stock cook at a steady simmer. After about 15 minutes, the rice should have swelled and become somewhat tender but still a bit hard in the middle. Continue adding stock for another few minutes, as needed, until the rice is plump, offers only the slightest resistance to the bite, and there is just enough thickened, creamy, saucelike broth to moisten the rice.

Season with salt and pepper and serve.

MAKES 4 TO 6 SERVINGS.

Saverio Pastor, a woodworker who makes forcole, *the oarlocks for gondolas*

RISOTTO WITH SEA SCALLOPS AND SAFFRON

*S*tarting in the 11th century, the spice trade with the East and with Africa enriched the coffers of the Venetian republic and its merchants. At one time there was an official Office of Saffron to control this precious spice, which comes from the stamens of the purple autumn crocus (three filaments per flower). Saffron may be associated with Spanish cooking, but it is also essential in the foods of northern Italy, where the saffron-tinted risotto alla milanese is a classic example. In discussing the Venetian love of color, Alexandre Dumas père asked

3 tablespoons (45 g) unsalted butter

½ cup (60 g) finely chopped onion

1½ teaspoons grated fresh ginger

1½ cups (250 g) vialone nano or arborio rice

⅓ cup (80 ml) dry white wine

½ teaspoon saffron threads

5 cups (1.25 l) hot vegetable stock
  (approximately) (recipe on page 85)

1 pound (500 g) sea scallops, cut in ¾-inch
  (2-cm) pieces (large bay scallops may
  be substituted)

Salt and freshly ground black pepper to taste

in his Grande Dictionnaire de la Cuisine *whether it was "to spices that we owe Titian's masterpieces" and answered, "I am tempted to believe it."*

Francesco's saffron risotto is seasoned with ginger and enriched with sea scallops for a voluptuous, golden dish. Despite its taste of the sea and its color, Francesco says it is modern rather than traditionally Venetian.

Heat the butter in a heavy 3-quart (3-l) saucepan. Add the onion and fresh ginger and sauté over medium heat until the onion is translucent but not brown. Add the rice and cook, stirring, until it begins to whiten. Stir in the wine and allow the mixture to simmer until most of the wine has evaporated.

Place the saffron in a small dish and pour 1 cup (250 ml) of the hot stock over it. Set aside for a few minutes. Have the rest of the stock simmering in a separate saucepan.

After the wine has evaporated, stir in ½ cup (125 ml) of the vegetable stock and continue to cook the rice mixture, stirring, until most of the liquid has been absorbed. Keep the mixture at a steady simmer. Stir in the cup of stock with the saffron and stir until most of the liquid has evaporated. Continue adding stock, a couple of ladles at a time, stirring and adding more as the stock is absorbed by the rice. Regulate the heat so the rice and stock cook at a steady simmer. After about 15 minutes, the rice should have swelled and become somewhat tender but still a bit hard in the middle. There should still be some stock left at this point.

Add the scallops. Stir, then continue adding stock for another few minutes, as needed, until the rice is plump, offers only the slightest resistance to the bite, and there is just enough thickened, creamy, saucelike broth to moisten the rice.

Season with salt and pepper and serve at once.

MAKES 6 SERVINGS.

JACOPO'S RISOTTO

*T*his is one of the recipes that Francesco remembers his mother preparing for him when he was a child and that he now makes for his little son, Jacopo. It's simply risotto with milk. But add some butter and Parmesan cheese and it becomes sophisticated enough for adult meals. Spread the risotto in a baking dish and gratinée it with bread crumbs to transform it into a deliciously simple accompaniment for roasted meats.

"The one thing you have to remember about making risotto for children," says Francesco, "is that you want it soft, not al dente." For that reason, the proportion of liquid to rice in this recipe is larger than usual. Another clever kitchen tip is to keep a metal spoon in the pot while the milk is heating. It prevents the milk from boiling over.

INGREDIENTS

1 cup (150 g) arborio rice

2 cups (500 ml) regular or low-fat milk

4 cups (1 l) water

Salt and freshly ground black pepper to taste

2 tablespoons (30 g) unsalted butter

¼ cup (30 g) freshly grated Parmesan cheese (optional)

⅓ cup (45 g) dry bread crumbs (optional)

Place the rice and 1 cup (250 ml) of the milk in a heavy saucepan. Over low heat, gradually bring the milk to a boil. To keep the milk from boiling over, place a metal spoon in the pan as the milk is heating.

Remove the metal spoon and, stirring the rice, gradually add the remaining milk. After all the milk has been incorporated, gradually add the water, about ½ cup (125 ml) at a time, stirring constantly. The rice should be very tender after about 20 to 25 minutes. Season it with salt and pepper.

Stir in the butter and, if desired, the cheese and serve. At this point, if desired, the rice can be spread in a buttered flameproof baking dish and topped with the bread crumbs. Just before serving, place the dish under a broiler to brown the top lightly.

MAKES 4 SERVINGS.

POLENTA WITH CUTTLEFISH SAUCE

*A*mericans think of squid and its ink as the essential ingredients to make the black sauce that is served in Venice with polenta, risotto, or pasta. But Francesco points out that the sea creature with the most ink is the cuttlefish, which is a little larger than squid. Many fish markets sell cleaned squid; some sell cuttlefish. If cuttlefish is not available, squid can be substituted. Lately, some specialty food stores have started carrying little packets of cuttlefish ink to use for making these recipes. "I don't entirely trust them," Francesco says. "I'm not sure what they have put in those packets."

Heat the oil in a large, heavy skillet. Add the onion and garlic and cook until they are tender but not brown.

Stir in the cuttlefish or squid and cook over medium heat about 30 minutes, until all the liquid from the cuttlefish or squid has evaporated.

Meanwhile, force the tomatoes through a food mill and mix with the juice from the tomatoes and the ink. Set aside.

When the liquid has evaporated in the skillet, stir in the wine and cook until the wine has evaporated and the mixture in the skillet is beginning to color. Stir in the tomato and ink mixture, add the water, and cook gently another 45 minutes to I hour, until the cuttlefish or squid is tender, adding a little more water if necessary during cooking. Season with salt and pepper.

Prepare the polenta and serve topped with the cuttlefish or squid and its sauce.

MAKES 6 SERVINGS.

INGREDIENTS

3 tablespoons (45 ml) extra virgin olive oil

½ cup (60 g) chopped onion

I clove garlic

I½ pounds (750 g) cleaned cuttlefish or
    squid, sliced in rings

4 fresh or canned peeled plum (egg) tomatoes

½ cup (125 ml) juice from the tomatoes

I½ teaspoons cuttlefish or squid ink

⅓ cup (80 ml) dry white wine

I cup (250 ml) water (approximately)

Salt and freshly ground black pepper to taste

Basic soft white polenta (recipe on page 68)

POLENTA WITH WILD MUSHROOMS

INGREDIENTS

4 ounces (125 g) dried porcini mushrooms

8 ounces (250 g) fresh oyster mushrooms

8 ounces (250 g) shiitake mushrooms, roasted
(recipe on page 96)

3 tablespoons (45 ml) extra virgin olive oil

4 cloves garlic, chopped fine

1 tablespoon fresh rosemary leaves

Salt and freshly ground black pepper to taste

1 tablespoon chopped flat-leaf (Italian) parsley

Basic soft yellow polenta (recipe below)

The pairing of creamy polenta with a ragout of earthy wild mushrooms has to be one of the glories of northern Italian cooking. Mid-autumn, when a profusion of wild mushrooms begins to appear in the Rialto market, is the best time to prepare this dish in Venice. "Now you have all these mushrooms all the time in America," Francesco says. So he's happy to be able to prepare polenta with wild (or exotic) mushrooms any time.

Place the dried porcini in a bowl, cover with warm water, and set aside to soak for 1 hour. Drain and pat dry on paper towels.

Cut any very large oyster mushrooms into 1½- to 2-inch (4- to 5-cm) pieces. Cut any very large shiitake mushrooms into halves or quarters.

Heat the oil in a large, heavy skillet. Add all the mushrooms and the garlic and sauté over medium heat until they are lightly browned and tender, about 10 minutes. Halfway through the cooking, add the rosemary. Season with salt and pepper, stir in the parsley, and set aside while preparing the polenta.

When the polenta is done, briefly reheat the mushroom mixture and serve hot over the hot polenta.

MAKES 6 SERVINGS.

BASIC SOFT POLENTA

"In different regions of the North, we have different kinds of polenta," Francesco explains. "In Bergamo they make it very firm. In Venice it's often white, made with white cornmeal, which is more refined but takes longer to cook. Polenta is really food for the poor. In poor families with lots of children you would be served a big polenta for dinner with one sausage sitting in the middle." Francesco also says that most people make polenta starting with boiling water. You can also start it in cold water, which is easier, "but you have to bring it to a boil very fast," he says. Use a little less water if the polenta is meant to be firmer so it can be spread in a pan, allowed to cool, then cut in rectangles to grill or sauté.

INGREDIENTS

6 cups (1.5 l) water

Sea salt

1½ cups (220 g) yellow or white cornmeal
for polenta, preferably stone-ground

¼ cup (60 g) unsalted butter

Bring the water to a boil in a heavy saucepan. Add about a teaspoon of salt.

Very gradually add the polenta by taking handfuls of it and letting it fall in a thin stream into the pan. Stir it constantly.

After all the polenta has been added, continue to cook it, stirring, for 10 minutes. Add the butter, season to taste with salt, and serve.

MAKES 6 SERVINGS.

Polenta with Wild Mushrooms

1 pound (500 g) spaghetti

Salt

6 oven-dried tomatoes, seeded and chopped
    (recipe on page 71)

6 large cloves roasted garlic, peeled
    (recipe on page 71)

¼ cup (60 ml) extra virgin olive oil, or more,
    to taste

24 fresh basil leaves

Freshly ground black pepper

Pinch of hot red pepper flakes

SPAGHETTI WITH OVEN-DRIED TOMATOES

"*I think oven-dried tomatoes make the best spaghetti sauce in the world.*" *Francesco prefers to oven-dry regular round tomatoes, not the oval plum or Roma variety, which he finds can taste too aggressive and overpower the pasta. "I also like the bright flavor of this pasta better without cheese, which adds a pungency it does not need," he says. "You should not automatically put cheese on every pasta; it depends on the flavors." This pasta can be served hot or at room temperature.*

Bring a large pot of water to a boil, add salt, then add the spaghetti. Cook until it is al dente, about 8 minutes, then drain it well.

While the spaghetti is cooking, combine the tomatoes, garlic, and olive oil in a very large, heavy skillet. Cook over medium heat a few minutes, then add the drained spaghetti. Toss the spaghetti and tomatoes together for several minutes, add the basil, season with salt and pepper, and add the hot red pepper flakes.

Remove from the heat, add a little more olive oil if desired, then serve.

MAKES 4 TO 6 SERVINGS.

OVEN-DRIED TOMATOES

Chefs have largely abandoned the Italian tradition of canning tomatoes or cooking them in a pot on top of the stove to make sauces for pasta, and with good reason. They find there is too much liquid, which dilutes the flavor. Instead they roast the tomatoes in the oven for several hours, causing the excess moisture to evaporate and giving the tomatoes, especially the ones that are not picked fresh from the vine in midsummer, a richer, more concentrated taste. "When you have really ripe tomatoes, you taste the sun in your mouth," Francesco says. "And with oven-dried tomatoes you always have a good tomato flavor."

INGREDIENTS

24 ripe tomatoes

6 to 8 sprigs fresh rosemary

6 to 8 sprigs fresh thyme

½ teaspoon sugar

Salt to taste

Preheat the oven to 250°F (120°C). Line a large baking sheet with parchment paper.

Slice the top ¼ to ½ inch (6 to 13 mm) off each tomato. Sprinkle each with pieces of rosemary and thyme, the sugar, and salt.

Place in the oven and roast about 3 hours, until the tomatoes are cooked but still hold their shape.

Slip off the skins and use in a recipe or freeze loosely packed in 1-quart (1-l) containers until ready to use. While still frozen, the cooked tomatoes can be scooped out one at a time, as needed, from the containers.

MAKES ABOUT 4 QUARTS (4 L).

ROASTED GARLIC

INGREDIENTS

1 head garlic

2 cups (500 g) kosher salt (approximately)

Roasting garlic tenderizes and mellows it. The roasted heads can be kept refrigerated for several days. Burying the garlic in salt to roast it is utterly Venetian.

Preheat the oven to 350°F (180°C).

Place the unpeeled head of garlic in a small baking dish and cover it completely with the salt. Place in the oven and roast for about 45 minutes.

Remove the garlic from the salt and refrigerate it until ready to use.

MAKES 1 HEAD ROASTED GARLIC.

FUSILLI WITH RADICCHIO

*T**his is a typically Venetian recipe that Francesco brought from home. "I did not serve it in Remi at first," he says, "because I was afraid it was not really to the American taste." But the combination of the bitter radicchio with the slightly smoky bacon smoothed with a bit of butter and cheese is irresistible and now has a permanent place on the menu.*

INGREDIENTS

Salt

1 tablespoon extra virgin olive oil

4 ounces (125 g) Canadian bacon, diced

3 heads radicchio, cored and shredded

1 pound (500 g) fusilli

1 tablespoon unsalted butter

Freshly grated Parmesan cheese

Bring a large pot of salted water to a boil for the fusilli.

Meanwhile, heat the oil in a large, heavy skillet. Add the bacon and sauté over medium heat until it just begins to brown. Add the radicchio and stir-fry for a few minutes, until it begins to wilt. Add a few tablespoons water and continue to cook the radicchio and bacon together until the radicchio is tender.

When the water for the pasta is boiling, add the fusilli and cook it about 8 minutes, until it is al dente. Drain it well, then transfer it to the skillet with the radicchio and bacon and toss them together. Add the butter.

Serve at once with grated cheese on the side.

MAKES 4 SERVINGS.

Double recipe *zucchini in umido*, without mint
   or cheese (page 101)

1 slender zucchini (courgette), sliced
   paper thin

1 cup (250 ml) extra virgin olive oil or
   vegetable oil

Salt

12 ounces (375 g) fresh fettuccine (dried
   penne or linguine may be used)

1 tablespoon unsalted butter

Freshly ground black pepper to taste

1 tablespoon chopped flat-leaf (Italian) parsley

2 ounces (60 g) fresh Parmesan cheese, in
   paper-thin shavings

FETTUCCINE WITH STEWED ZUCCHINI

This recipe consists essentially of Francesco's lush, simple stewed zucchini (zucchini in umido) tossed with fresh fettuccine and garnished with crisp slices of fried zucchini and shavings of Parmesan cheese.

Prepare the *zucchini in umido* and set aside to keep warm.

Pat the slices of zucchini dry on paper towels. Heat the oil in a heavy skillet and fry the zucchini slices until they are golden brown. Drain on absorbent paper.

Bring a large pot of salted water to a boil for the pasta. Add the fettuccine, stir, and cook about 2 minutes. Drain the pasta and toss in a warm bowl with the butter and salt and pepper. (Penne or linguine will take about 6 minutes to cook.)

Reheat the *zucchini in umido*, add to the pasta, and toss again. Serve, topping each serving with a sprinkling of parsley, some cheese shavings, and slices of fried zucchini.

MAKES 4 SERVINGS.

LINGUINE WITH BROCCOLI RABE, CLAMS, AND HOT PEPPER

INGREDIENTS

3 tablespoons (45 ml) extra virgin olive oil

3 cloves garlic

½ bunch broccoli rabe, stems removed, chopped

8 ounces (250 g) cockles, Manila or
    littleneck clams

8 ounces (250 g) linguine

Hot red pepper flakes to taste

Although this is a dish one can find in Venice today, it is essentially a recipe from the south, around Naples. "Things move around more now than they did when I was growing up," Francesco says. "And with the wonderful clams we have in Venice, there's no reason we shouldn't enjoy a dish like this." Although clams are delicious when steamed open in white wine, Francesco does not use wine in a sauce for pasta because he finds it makes the pasta taste sour. "The water from cooking the pasta is a better liquid to use," he advises.

Bring a pot with 4 quarts (4 l) of water to a boil for the linguine.

Meanwhile heat the oil in a heavy 3-quart (3-l) saucepan. Add the garlic, cook for a minute, then stir in the broccoli rabe. When the rabe has wilted, stir in the clams, cover, and cook over low heat until they have opened, about 10 minutes.

When the water for the linguine is boiling, add the pasta, stir it, and cook until it is al dente, about 8 minutes. Drain the pasta, reserving about 2 cups (500 ml) of the cooking water, and return the pasta to the pot.

Stir about a cup (250 ml) of the pasta cooking liquid in with the clams, then transfer the clams and broccoli rabe to the pot with the linguine. Mix the ingredients well. Add more liquid from the linguine if necessary. Sprinkle with hot red pepper flakes and serve.

MAKES 2 TO 4 SERVINGS.

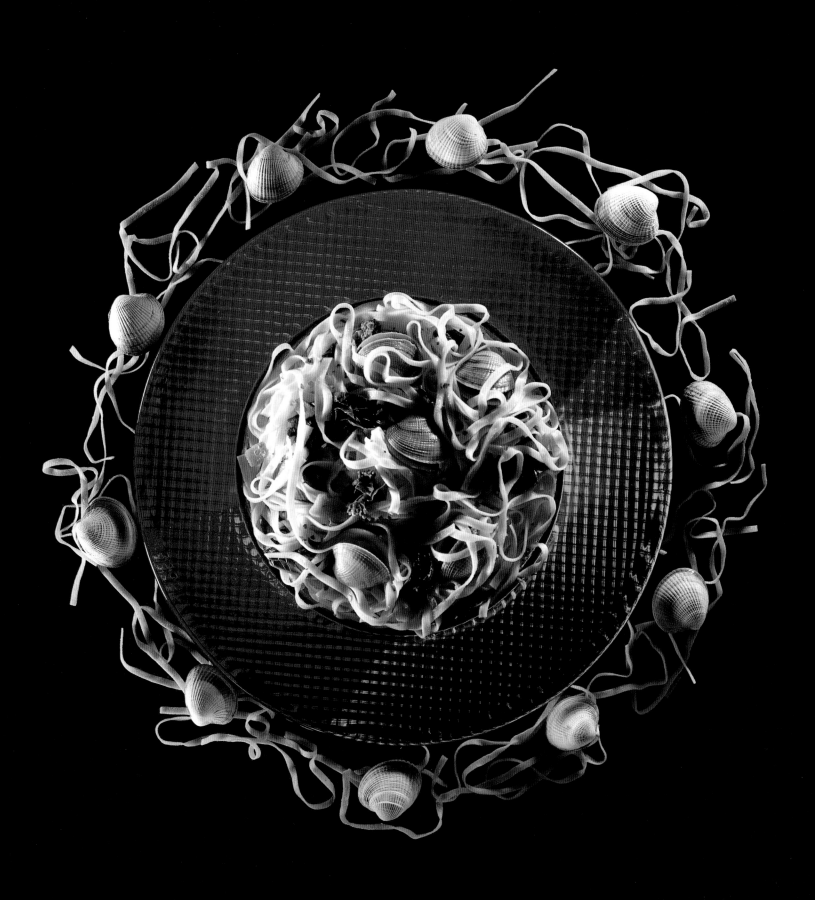

JACOPO'S SPAGHETTI WITH TUNA (SPAGHETTI ALLA CORSARA)

INGREDIENTS

8 ounces (250 g) spaghetti

1 6½-ounce (200-g) can tuna in olive oil

3 tablespoons (22 g) freshly grated Parmesan cheese (optional)

1 cup (250 g) chopped fresh, canned, or oven-dried tomato (optional)

2 cloves garlic, finely chopped (optional)

2 tablespoons finely chopped flat-leaf (Italian) parsley (optional)

This children's dish, one that Francesco's little son, Jacopo, loves, consists simply of spaghetti mixed with mashed canned tuna. Francesco recommends using Italian tuna canned in olive oil. "For grownups you can turn it into pirate spaghetti—spaghetti alla corsara— by adding a little tomato, parsley, and garlic," Francesco says. "But to tell the truth, I like eating it plain, with my son."

Bring a large pot of water to a boil, add the spaghetti, and cook it until it is al dente, about 8 minutes.

While the spaghetti is cooking, mash the tuna with a fork.

When the spaghetti is done, spoon off a few tablespoons of the cooking water and reserve them, then drain the spaghetti.

Transfer the spaghetti to a large bowl and toss it with the tuna, using the reserved water to moisten the mixture if necessary. If desired, add the Parmesan cheese and serve.

To make *spaghetti alla corsara*, add the tomato, garlic, and parsley to the spaghetti with the tuna, toss the ingredients well, and serve hot or at room temperature.

MAKES 3 TO 4 SERVINGS.

BIGOLI WITH ANCHOVIES AND ONIONS

"This is a very traditional pasta, but as simple as it is, you have to be careful with the seasoning or the balance of flavors will be destroyed." Francesco says that in Venice it is often eaten around Easter time, at the end of Lent. Bigoli is commercial whole wheat (wholemeal) pasta that comes in thick strands. Whole wheat linguine or spaghetti can be substituted.

Purée the anchovies with the water in a blender or mash them with a fork and mix them with the warm water. Set aside.

Heat the oil in a large, heavy skillet. Add the onions and cook, stirring, over medium heat until they are golden. Stir in the anchovy purée and set aside.

Bring a large pot of water to a boil, add the bigoli, stir, and cook about 8 minutes, until the bigoli is al dente. Drain it well.

Transfer the pasta to the skillet with the onions and anchovies and reheat gently, tossing to mix all the ingredients. Fold in the parsley, season with salt and pepper, and serve.

MAKES 4 TO 6 SERVINGS.

INGREDIENTS

10 to 12 anchovy fillets (the meatier, the better), drained

½ cup (125 ml) warm water

¼ cup (60 ml) extra virgin olive oil

2 large onions, sliced thin

1 pound (500 g) bigoli

2 tablespoons coarsely chopped flat-leaf (Italian) parsley

Salt and freshly ground black pepper to taste

BIGOLI WITH DUCK AND RADICCHIO

INGREDIENTS

1 duck breast (2 halves), or 1½ cups (250 g) diced cooked duck

1 tablespoon extra virgin olive oil

2 heads radicchio, cored and slivered

1 cup (250 ml) dry red wine

1 cup (250 ml) duck demi-glace

Salt and freshly ground black pepper to taste

1 pound (500 g) bigoli (see note, preceding recipe)

Freshly grated Parmesan cheese

"Most people would not think of a dish like this as Venetian," Francesco says, "but there is nothing more Venetian than eating birds with radicchio and bigoli." In Remi there is plenty of duck on hand to use for making this dish. Home cooks who cannot obtain duck breasts should remember this dish when they make roast duck because it works beautifully with leftovers. If your market sells cooked duck or duck confit, it can also be used.

This recipe calls for demi-glace, a thick, concentrated stock. For those who do not make stocks at home, it is sold in some fancy food shops. As a substitute, a mixture of salt-free chicken and beef broths can be boiled down until it is syrupy and thick.

Preheat the oven to 400°F (200°C). Place a baking dish in the oven to preheat. Place the duck breast, skin side down, on the hot baking dish and cook it for about 20 minutes, until it is medium-rare.

Remove the duck from the oven, allow it to cool to room temperature, then remove the skin. Dice the duck meat. You should have about 1½ cups (250 g).

Heat the oil in a very large skillet, add the radicchio, and sauté until it begins to wilt. Add the wine and continue to cook the radicchio until it is tender and the wine has reduced by at least half, about 15 minutes. Stir in the demi-glace and duck meat, bring to a simmer, and cook 10 minutes longer. Season with salt and pepper.

Bring a large pot of salted water to a boil, add the bigoli, and cook until it is al dente, about 8 minutes. Drain the bigoli well, then transfer it to the skillet with the radicchio and duck. Toss the ingredients together over medium heat about 5 minutes, then serve. Pass the Parmesan cheese on the side.

MAKES 4 SERVINGS.

1½ cups (375 g) ricotta cheese

½ cup (125 g) fresh goat cheese

Pinch of grated nutmeg

3 large egg yolks

1 cup (125 g) freshly grated Parmesan cheese

Salt and freshly ground black pepper to taste

1¼ pounds (625 g) fresh pasta (recipe on page 82)

1 whole large egg beaten with 2 tablespoons (30 ml) water

Semolina

6 tablespoons (90 g) unsalted butter

18 fresh sage leaves

CHEESE RAVIOLI IN BROWN BUTTER AND SAGE

"American ricotta cheese tends to be very wet," Francesco complains. "I like to add some goat cheese to give it more body, but you can do whatever you want." This is ravioli at its simplest, dressed up for dinner in nutty brown butter and sage, a finishing touch that ennobles even store-bought cheese ravioli.

Place the ricotta in a fine sieve and allow the excess fluid to drain for about 1 hour. Mix the drained ricotta with the goat cheese, nutmeg, egg yolks, ⅔ cup (85 g) of the Parmesan cheese, salt, and pepper. Set aside.

Roll the fresh pasta into sheets and spread half the sheets on a work surface. Brush lightly with the egg-water wash and cut out 2½-inch (6.5-cm) rounds.

Spoon a mound of the cheese mixture onto each round, leaving at least a ½-inch (1.3-cm) border. Cut the rest of the pasta into 2½-inch (6.5-cm) rounds, place the rounds on top of the cheese mounds, then press the edges together by hand or with a fork. Dust lightly with semolina, cover, and refrigerate until just before serving.

Heat the butter in a skillet, add the sage leaves, and cook over medium heat until the butter is medium brown. Remove from the heat.

Just before serving, bring a pot of salted water to a boil, lower the heat to a simmer, and carefully slip the ravioli into the pot. Allow them to simmer a few minutes, until they rise to the surface. Drain them well.

Briefly reheat the butter and sage mixture. Divide the ravioli among 6 plates and spoon the butter sauce over each. Dust with the remaining Parmesan cheese.

MAKES 6 SERVINGS.

TUNA RAVIOLI WITH GINGER MARCO POLO

INGREDIENTS

1 tablespoon extra virgin olive oil

2 tablespoons finely chopped carrot

2 tablespoons finely chopped onion

2 tablespoons finely chopped fennel

1 teaspoon minced fresh ginger

12 ounces (375 g) raw fresh tuna, ground

¼ cup (60 g) ricotta cheese, well drained

Salt and freshly ground black pepper to taste

1¼ pounds (625 g) fresh pasta (recipe on page 82)

1 large egg yolk beaten with 2 tablespoons (30 ml) water

Semolina

2 tablespoons (30 ml) canola oil

1 2-inch (5-cm) piece peeled ginger, sliced paper thin

¼ cup (60 g) unsalted butter

1 cup (250 g) chopped fresh, oven-dried, or well-drained canned tomato

¼ cup (60 ml) fish stock (recipe on page 86) or water

1 teaspoon fresh tarragon leaves

This could be considered the signature dish at Remi, created by Francesco Antonucci but inspired by Adam Tihany. Ravioli filled with fresh tuna is spiced, Marco Polo style, with fresh ginger. "This might be the most exotic dish in the restaurant," Francesco says. Actually, the Romans had ginger, but then its cultivation disappeared. The Venetian Marco Polo reintroduced it to Europe in the 13th century. These intriguingly spicy ravioli are served in a light tomato sauce with frizzles of deep-fried ginger on top. Sheets of commercial pasta may be substituted for homemade.

Heat the oil in a heavy skillet, add the carrot, onion, fennel, and minced ginger, and sauté over medium heat until the vegetables are tender. Allow the mixture to cool briefly, then mix in the tuna and ricotta. Season with salt and pepper.

Spread 3 sheets of fresh pasta on a lightly floured work surface. Place slightly rounded tablespoonfuls of the filling 2 inches (5 cm) apart on the pasta. Brush some of the yolk-water wash around each mound of filling. Cover with the remaining pasta and, using a ravioli cutter or a knife, cut squares around the mounds of filling. Seal the edges by hand or with the tines of a fork. Arrange them on a platter and dust them with semolina so they do not stick. Refrigerate until ready to serve.

Heat the canola oil in a heavy skillet. Add the ginger and fry it over medium-high heat until it is lightly browned.

In a separate pan, melt the butter over medium heat. Add the tomato and stock, cook for 5 minutes, then add the tarragon. Season with salt and pepper.

Bring a large pot of water to a boil, add the ravioli, reduce the heat, and simmer about 6 minutes. Drain, then divide the ravioli among 6 plates. Reheat the tomato sauce and spoon some of it over each portion. Top with fried ginger and serve.

Photograph on page 6.

MAKES 6 SERVINGS.

FRESH PASTA FOR RAVIOLI

What is a simple, almost everyday task in Italy can be a major production in other countries. But once successfully made, fresh pasta dough can become a habit. The recipe can be cut in half. "It's important to try to make the dough on a humid day so it does not dry out," Francesco says. He uses a blend of all-purpose and semolina flours because he finds the addition of the semolina makes the dough a little easier to handle.

Mix the semolina and all-purpose flour together and place in a mound on a work surface. Make a well in the center.

Beat the eggs together and carefully pour them into the center of the well. Using a fork, gradually work the flour mixture from the inside of the well into the egg mixture, taking care not to break the walls of the well and allow the egg to run out. Continue mixing eggs and flours together until the egg has become fairly thick. Then, using your hands, incorporate all the egg and flour together, kneading them until they are smooth.

Roll the dough out by hand or run it through progressively finer settings on a pasta machine to make thin sheets. When the sheets of dough have been made, keep them moist by covering them with a barely damp towel.

Cut into noodles or fill for ravioli. Cook and serve or refrigerate or freeze until ready to serve. Noodles can also be allowed to dry.

MAKES ABOUT 1¼ POUNDS (625 G), ENOUGH FOR 6 SHEETS FOR RAVIOLI.

POTATO GNOCCHI

"It is essential to peel and mash the potatoes while they are very hot because you want them to be light and floury, not gluey," Francesco points out. *He prefers Idaho potatoes for these lovely, cloudlike gnocchi because they have a dry texture. To retain the starch, he does not peel them before boiling them.*

Place the potatoes in a saucepan, cover with water, and boil until they are tender, about 40 minutes.

Remove the potatoes from the pan and, protecting your hands with a clean towel, peel them. Mash them into a bowl using a potato ricer. Cover and set aside to cool about 15 minutes.

Make a well in the center of the potatoes and add the cheese, nutmeg, eggs, and egg yolk. Begin working them into the potatoes, gradually adding the flour and salt, until the mixture makes a soft dough that holds its shape well.

Using about a cup (250 g) of the dough at a time, roll the dough on a lightly floured board to make a rope about ¾ inch (2 cm) in diameter. Cut it into 1-inch (2.5-cm) lengths, then lightly imprint each piece with the tines of a fork.

To cook, bring a large pot of salted water to a boil. Lower the heat to a lively simmer and drop in 2 or 3 of the gnocchi to test the cooking time. Just after they rise to the surface, taste them. If they are too soft, remove the gnocchi from the boiling water sooner. If they are too firm, allow the gnocchi to cook longer. Cook the rest of the gnocchi, adding only as many to the pot as will not be crowded on the surface when they rise. You may have to cook them in several batches.

Drain the gnocchi and serve them with butter or a sauce. They can be allowed to cool, then reheated by plunging them into simmering water or baking them with a sauce.

MAKES ABOUT 1 ½ POUNDS (750 G), 4 TO 6 SERVINGS.

INGREDIENTS

4 Idaho (baking) potatoes

½ cup (60 g) grated Parmesan cheese

Pinch of grated nutmeg

2 large eggs, beaten

1 large egg yolk, beaten

1 cup (125 g) flour

Salt to taste

PUMPKIN GNOCCHI

INGREDIENTS

1½ pounds (750 g) peeled, seeded pumpkin
  or butternut squash, cubed

½ cup (60 g) freshly grated Parmesan cheese

½ teaspoon ground cinnamon

Salt and freshly ground black pepper to taste

2 large egg yolks, beaten

¾ cup (90 g) flour (approximately)

3 tablespoons (45 g) unsalted butter or truffle
  butter (if available)

These richly flavored yet delicate gnocchi are typical of dishes from the region around Venice. The recipe that follows is one that Dario Plozer, one of Francesco's sous chefs, learned from his mother in Udine. "A dish like this is a frustration for me," Francesco says. "It's really too delicate to make in a restaurant and should be prepared at home."

Preheat the oven to 350°F (180°C). Spread the pumpkin in a baking dish, cover, and bake until tender, about 20 minutes. Mash it into a bowl.

Mix the mashed pumpkin with half the cheese and all the cinnamon. Season with salt and pepper. Beat in the egg yolks and stir in the flour, adding enough flour to make a soft dough.

Pack the mixture into a pastry bag fitted with a plain ½-inch (1.3-cm) tube. Bring a pot of salted water to a simmer. Force the pumpkin mixture through the pastry bag, cutting off 1-inch (2.5-cm) lengths as it emerges from the bag and letting the pieces drop into the simmering water. The best way to do this is to rest the tip of the bag on the edge of the saucepan so you have one hand free to cut the gnocchi mixture as it comes out of the bag.

Simmer the gnocchi about 30 seconds. As they are cooked and rise to the surface, scoop them out of the saucepan and into a bowl of ice water. Drain them after they have been chilled.

To serve, reheat the gnocchi briefly in simmering water, drain them well, and serve tossed gently with plain or truffle butter. Dust with the remaining Parmesan cheese.

MAKES 2 FIRST COURSE OR
4 SIDE DISH SERVINGS.

VEGETABLE STOCK

INGREDIENTS

1 large carrot, peeled

2 stalks celery

1 large leek, rinsed and trimmed

1 onion, quartered

12 cups (3 l) cold water

Salt to taste

At Remi this vegetable stock is used as a base for many of the risottos, especially the ones made without meat or fish. "We have many people coming into the restaurant who are vegetarians," Francesco explains, "and we want to be able to accommodate them. When it's well made, a vegetable stock is full of flavor."

Place the vegetables in a small stockpot, add the water, bring to a simmer, and cook gently for 1 hour, until the liquid is reduced to 2 quarts (2 l). Skim off any surface foam from time to time.

Strain the stock, season lightly with salt, and allow to cool to room temperature. Refrigerate or freeze until ready to use.

MAKES 2 QUARTS (2 L).

SEAFOOD STOCK

INGREDIENTS

1 tablespoon extra virgin olive oil

¼ cup (30 g) chopped onion

1 stalk celery, chopped

½ carrot, peeled and chopped

Heads and shells of 2 small (1-pound/ 500-g) lobsters

⅓ cup (80 ml) dry white wine

3 tablespoons (45 ml) cognac or brandy

8 cups (2 l) fish stock (recipe on page 86)

This is the richest of the basic stocks in Francesco's repertory. Built on a base of fish stock, it makes a delicious risotto and a wonderful seafood stew. "The aroma makes me think of Venice and the Rialto market, where so much comes from the sea," he says. Obtaining the lobster heads and shells may require giving your fish market some advance notice. Otherwise, buy whole lobsters with the intention of using the meat in another recipe.

Heat the oil in a heavy stockpot. Add the onion and cook over low heat until it is soft but not brown, about 8 minutes. Stir in the celery and carrot and cook 5 minutes longer.

Stir in the lobster heads and shells and the wine and cook until nearly all the wine has evaporated. Add the cognac and cook until it has evaporated.

Stir in the fish stock and simmer 30 minutes, skimming the surface as needed. Strain, allow to cool to room temperature, then refrigerate or freeze.

MAKES 5 CUPS (1.25 L).

FISH STOCK

INGREDIENTS

Head and bones of a 4-pound (2-kg)
    white-fleshed fish

4 quarts (4 l) cold water

2 large carrots, peeled

2 stalks celery

1 onion, quartered

1 tomato

Salt to taste

"Fish and seafood are so important in Venice," says Francesco, "that when making fish stews and risottos with fish, we prefer a fish stock. For shrimp, lobster, and crabs a shellfish stock is better." None are complicated to prepare.

Place the fish head and bones in a large stockpot. Add the cold water, bring to a simmer, and cook for 5 minutes, skimming any foam from the surface.

Add the carrots, celery, onion, and tomato. Continue to simmer for 20 minutes.

Strain the stock, season lightly with salt, and allow to cool to room temperature. Refrigerate or freeze until ready to use.

MAKES 10 CUPS (2.5 L).

BASIL OIL

1 cup (about 40 g) loosely packed fresh
basil leaves

½ cup (about 20 g) loosely packed
curly parsley

½ cup (125 ml) extra virgin olive oil

Salt to taste

"*This basil oil is based on the same principle as pesto, but it's lighter, made without the garlic, cheese, and nuts,*" *Francesco says.* "*And it has more uses.*" *He adds droplets of the brightly colored oil to garnish the top of a simple risotto and to glaze grilled fish.* "*I like to combine parsley and basil to give it a more intense flavor, and this is the only time I use American-style curly parsley instead of the flat-leaf kind.*" *Francesco also blanches the herbs very briefly to mute any bitterness.* "*We serve very little in the way of raw food in Venice,*" *he remarks.* "*As a matter of fact, that's true of Italy in general, not just Venice.*"

Bring a pot with 2 quarts (2 l) of water to a boil, drop in the basil and parsley, and cook just 15 seconds. Drain immediately, rinse the herbs under cold water, and dry them.

Place the herbs in a blender or food processor. Process them to chop them, then, with the machine running, gradually add the oil. Season the mixture with salt.

MAKES ABOUT ⅔ CUP (160 ML).

Carrot Soup with Prosecco, recipe on page 91

V·E·G·E·T·A·B·L·E·S

Perhaps it is the particular light in Venice, but the vegetables on display in the Rialto market have uncommonly intense color. From the snowy heads of cauliflower and fennel, to the rich gold of pumpkins and the brilliant green of chard and broccoli rabe, to the scarlet of the tomatoes and intense burgundy of the ubiquitous radicchio, this is a painterly array.

The vegetables grown in the rich, loamy soil bordering the lagoon inform the menu today as they have since the early 14th century, when the farmlands of the Veneto, around Padua and Treviso, came under Venetian control. Today vegetables enliven the antipasto course, dress the risotto and pasta, and enhance all manner of seafood and meats.

Seasonal considerations prevail. The Venetians celebrate the first peas in April, a time when early asparagus and artichokes also vie for attention. Throughout the summer and into fall, when baskets of freshly dug mushrooms and shiny mahogany chestnuts appear, a dazzling abundance is on hand. And even in the damp, bone-chilling cold of winter, the shopper finds baroque squashes and pumpkins, cabbages and potatoes, and even the white-fleshed sweet potatoes Venetians call "American potatoes."

Like most of the foods in Venice, vegetables are treated with simple respect in cooking. They may be grilled, stewed in butter, puréed for soup, or mixed with rice. A handful of herbs and perhaps a shower of freshly grated Parmesan cheese are usually the only adornment they receive.

Most of Venice's vegetable varieties can be obtained in America and elsewhere. What poses a greater challenge is finding comparable flavor and quality. Whenever possible, buy vegetables from a farm stand or a farmer's market. Look for those that have been grown organically because they usually taste better. And if you go to market seeking asparagus, for example, and those that are available are not first-rate, choose a different vegetable to bake or use in the risotto. There are dozens of options.

Additional recipes made with vegetables can be found in other chapters:

ANTIPASTO

CARROT SOUP WITH PROSECCO

INGREDIENTS

¾ cup (90 g) chopped onions

2 tablespoons (30 ml) extra virgin olive oil

1 pound (500 g) carrots, peeled and
    coarsely chopped

1½ stalks celery, chopped

1 baking potato, peeled and diced

4½ cups (1.125 l) vegetable stock (recipe on
    page 85) or water

2 cups (500 ml) prosecco or other dry
    sparkling wine

2 bay leaves

Salt and freshly ground black pepper to taste

*F*rancesco's gentle, velvety carrot soup is given a touch of festive Venetian froth with a last-minute splash of prosecco, the dry sparkling wine of the Veneto. "The minute you taste prosecco, you have Venice in your mouth," Francesco likes to say.

Place the onions in a heavy 3-quart (3-l) saucepan. Stir in the oil, cover, and cook over low heat about 10 minutes, until they are soft but have not taken on any color.

Stir in the carrots, celery, and potato, cook for about a minute, then add the stock, 1¼ cups (310 ml) of the wine, and the bay leaves.

Simmer, partly covered, for about 30 minutes, until the vegetables are very tender. Remove the bay leaves.

Allow the mixture to cool briefly, then purée in a blender or food processor. You may have to do this in 2 batches. Strain the soup.

To serve, reheat the soup and season it with salt and pepper. Spoon it into 6 warm soup plates. At the table, pour 1½ to 2 tablespoons (20 to 30 ml) of chilled prosecco into each portion. The soup will froth up a bit.

Photograph on page 88.

MAKES 6 SERVINGS.

3 tablespoons (45 ml) extra virgin olive oil

½ cup (60 g) chopped onion

4 cups (500 g) diced fresh fennel

2 cups (250 g) diced celery root

10 cups (2.5 l) vegetable stock (recipe on page 85)

2 baking potatoes, peeled and cubed

½ teaspoon ground cumin

1 small lobster, about 1¼ pounds (625 g)

3 tablespoons (45 ml) Pernod or other anise-flavored spirits

Salt to taste

2 tablespoons chopped fresh tarragon

FENNEL SOUP WITH LOBSTER

*F*ennel, with its tantalizing anise flavor, is the basis for this smooth, elegant vegetable purée. So intrigued with fennel was Henry Wotten, England's ambassador to Venice in the 17th century, that he sent seeds to King James's gardener, with instructions on how they should be planted and the vegetable prepared. This soup is given a luxurious touch with the addition of lobster. "In Venice we would probably use scampi, but those are very difficult to find in America," Francesco says. "Besides, the lobsters here are wonderful, so this adaptation makes sense." At Remi, Francesco might replace the lobster with a dollop of crème fraîche topped with good sturgeon caviar, a special occasion touch that would not be out of place for a gala dinner at home.

Heat the oil in a heavy 4-quart (4-l) saucepan. Add the onion and fennel and cook slowly until they are transparent. Stir in the celery root.

Add the stock, bring to a simmer, and add the potatoes and cumin. Simmer, partly covered, for 45 minutes, until the vegetables are very tender.

While the vegetables are simmering, steam the lobster for 15 minutes. Allow it to cool slightly, then remove the claw meat and tail meat from the shells. Dice the lobster meat and set aside.

When the vegetables are tender, allow the soup to cool briefly, then purée it in a blender or food processor. You will have to do this in batches.

Return the soup to the saucepan, add the Pernod, and season with salt. Reheat the soup and stir in half the tarragon. To serve, spoon the soup into flat soup plates and spoon some of the lobster in the middle of each. Sprinkle with the remaining tarragon.

MAKES 6 SERVINGS.

CAULIFLOWER SOUP

"*In Venice we have big soups, simple soups,*" *Francesco says. "This is a good example." But he adds that when it's served at Remi, it is sometimes garnished with crème fraîche and caviar, for a lavish touch befitting the Venetian taste for luxury. At one time there were sturgeon in the Venetian lagoon, providing the city with its own supply of caviar. For a more humble Venetian garnish, some rounds of bread fried in butter or olive oil will do nicely.*

INGREDIENTS

5 tablespoons (45 g) unsalted butter

I small onion, chopped

I leek, chopped (white part only)

I baking potato, peeled and coarsely chopped

I small head or ½ large head cauliflower, coarsely chopped

I anchovy fillet, rinsed and chopped

8 cups (2 l) cold water

Salt and freshly ground white pepper to taste

4 3-inch (7.5-cm) rounds Italian country bread

Heat 2 tablespoons of the butter in a large, heavy saucepan. Add the onion and leek and sauté slowly until they are tender but not brown.

Add the potato, cauliflower, anchovy, and water. Bring to a simmer and cook, uncovered, for I hour. Allow the soup to cool briefly, then purée it in a blender or food processor. You will probably have to do this in batches.

Return the soup to the saucepan, bring it to a simmer, and season it with salt and white pepper.

Just before serving time, heat the remaining butter in a small skillet. Sauté the bread slices on both sides until they are golden and serve them alongside the soup.

MAKES 4 SERVINGS.

ARTICHOKES IN HERB SAUCE

Before Francesco handles artichokes, he rubs lemon all over his hands. "This is the way I learned to keep the artichokes from darkening," he says. It is actually more effective than merely rubbing the artichokes with lemon after they have been cut. In this recipe the artichokes are baked until tender and served in a richly verdant, garlicky herb sauce, a typically Venetian preparation. In Rome artichokes are fried, but in Venice the taste is for carciofi alla veneziana, *baby artichokes stewed in olive oil.*

INGREDIENTS

1 lemon

48 baby artichokes

2 cups (500 ml) water

4 cloves garlic, peeled

1 cup (45 g) flat-leaf (Italian) parsley,
    stems removed

1 cup (45 g) fresh basil leaves

3 tablespoons (45 ml) extra virgin olive oil

¼ cup (30 g) dry bread crumbs

3 tablespoons (22 g) freshly grated
    Parmesan cheese

Salt and freshly ground black pepper to taste

Cut the lemon in half, run the cut surface over your hands, then trim the artichokes. Juice the lemon and toss the artichokes in the lemon juice.

Preheat the oven to 400°F (200°C).

Bring the water to a simmer, add the garlic cloves, and cook 3 minutes. Add the parsley and basil and cook 2 minutes longer, then drain, reserving the liquid.

Mix the artichokes with the olive oil in a heavy casserole or shallow ovenproof saucepan. Add the garlic, parsley, basil, bread crumbs, and Parmesan cheese. Stir in ¾ cup (180 ml) of the liquid reserved from blanching the herbs and garlic. Cover and bake for 30 minutes.

Remove from the oven and separate the artichokes from the other ingredients. Set the artichokes aside. Remove and discard 3 of the garlic cloves, then purée the remaining herb mixture, adding another ½ cup (125 ml) reserved liquid. Season with salt and pepper. Pour the sauce over the artichokes and serve warm or at room temperature.

MAKES 6 SERVINGS.

ROASTED SHIITAKE MUSHROOMS

INGREDIENTS

12 ounces (375 g) shiitake mushrooms
(about 24 mushrooms)

2 tablespoons (30 ml) extra virgin olive oil

¼ cup (60 ml) dry white wine

Sprigs fresh rosemary, sage, and thyme

2 cloves garlic, sliced

Roasting vegetables, which concentrates their flavor by allowing excess moisture to evaporate, is one of the superb techniques that Francesco shares with many other contemporary chefs. Treating mushrooms in this manner results in luscious, meaty caps that are excellent served in salads. Roasted mushrooms can be sautéed quickly without flooding the pan with liquid, and when they are grilled they never turn tough.

Preheat the oven to 350°F (180°C). Line a baking pan with foil.

Remove the stems from the mushrooms and wipe off any dirt with a damp towel.

Sprinkle the oil and wine over the baking pan. Scatter the herbs and garlic on the pan, then place the mushrooms, brown side down, on top.

Bake for 10 minutes, turn the mushrooms, and bake 20 minutes longer.

Serve or use in other recipes.

MAKES 4 SERVINGS.

MUSTARD POTATOES

Francesco calls these sour potatoes—in Venetian, patate all'agro. *Something is lost in translation. In the Veneto the notion of a "sour" flavor has none of the negative connotations that it does in English. In fact, it implies a taste that is lively, appealing, and appetite-whetting.*

These "sour potatoes," or mustard potatoes as they are called at Remi, are a delicious addition to a cold summer buffet. The sauce is like a mayonnaise, made with raw egg yolks. When organic or farm eggs are used, the yolks should be safe to eat raw. If you have any doubt you can substitute 1½ cups (375 g) commercial mayonnaise thinned with the tarragon vinegar and stock and seasoned with the mustard and red onions.

INGREDIENTS

3 baking potatoes

2 tablespoons (30 g) Dijon mustard

2 raw egg yolks

2 tablespoons (30 ml) tarragon vinegar

Pinch of salt

1½ cups (375 ml) grapeseed or canola oil

¼ cup (30 g) very finely chopped red onion

⅓ cup (80 ml) vegetable stock (recipe on page 85) or water

1 tablespoon chopped flat-leaf (Italian) parsley

Steam the potatoes in their skins until they are tender, about 40 minutes. Peel and slice them ¼ inch (6 mm) thick.

Place the slices in a single layer on a baking sheet or one or more platters.

Combine the mustard, egg yolks, vinegar, and salt in a food processor and process until blended. With the machine running, slowly add the oil through the feed tube and process until the mixture is thick. Stir in the onion and the stock or water and beat until smooth.

Pour the dressing over the potatoes and allow to marinate ½ hour. Sprinkle with parsley before serving.

MAKES 4 TO 6 SERVINGS.

MASHED PARMESAN POTATOES

INGREDIENTS

4 Idaho (baking) potatoes, scrubbed

1½ tablespoons (20 g) butter, softened

1½ cups (375 ml) half and half (half cream
and half milk)

¼ cup (30 g) freshly grated Parmesan cheese,
or more, to taste

Salt and freshly ground white pepper to taste

These mashed potatoes are a simple, luxurious indulgence. They are rich enough to enjoy in small portions. There are lessons to be learned in the care with which Francesco selects and handles ingredients, including the everyday potato. His scrutiny of raw materials is typically Venetian. Shoppers in the Rialto market are extremely demanding and often wind up discussing the fish or produce with the seller or with perfect strangers.

"Idaho potatoes are the ones I prefer for mashing," says Francesco, "because they have a light, dry texture. But it is important to cook them unpeeled to keep the starch in and then peel and mash them while they are steaming hot, before they become glutinous, even at the risk of burning your fingers." He uses a clean towel—a chef's answer for a pot holder—to cradle the potatoes and protect his hands as he peels them. And an old-fashioned ricer, the kind of gadget that forces the potato through little holes, is best for mashing.

Boil or steam the potatoes until they are tender.

As soon as they are done, peel and mash them, preferably in a ricer. Mix in the butter with a fork.

Heat the half and half until bubbles begin to form around the edges, then add it to the potatoes, mixing well. Mix in the Parmesan cheese and season with salt and white pepper.

Serve at once or transfer to a buttered casserole, dust with additional cheese, and reheat for 15 minutes in a 350°F (180°C) oven.

See photograph on page 134.

Makes 6 servings.

MELANZANE FUNGHETTO

INGREDIENTS

1 large eggplant (aubergine)

¼ cup (60 ml) extra virgin olive oil

2 cloves garlic

Salt to taste

Hot red pepper flakes to taste

"*When you cook slices of eggplant that are mostly skin,*" Francesco explains, "*they come out looking like sautéed mushrooms, which is why this dish is called eggplant mushrooms.*"

Quarter the eggplant lengthwise and cut away the flesh to within ½ inch (1.3 cm) of the skin. Save the flesh from the center for another use or discard it. Cut the remaining eggplant with skin into little slivers.

Heat the oil in a large, heavy skillet or a wok. Add the eggplant and garlic and stir-fry until the eggplant is lightly browned, about 15 minutes. Season with salt and hot red pepper flakes and serve.

MAKES 4 TO 6 SERVINGS.

1 eggplant (aubergine), about 1¼ pounds (625 g)

⅓ cup (80 ml) extra virgin olive oil (approximately)

1 large onion, sliced ¼ inch (6 mm) thick

2 large cloves garlic, peeled

2 large red bell peppers (capsicums) or 1 red and 1 yellow pepper, seeded and cut into julienne strips

6 ounces (185 g) zucchini (courgettes), sliced ¼ inch (6 mm) thick

1 cup (250 g) crushed well-drained canned plum (egg) tomatoes

Salt and freshly ground black pepper to taste

Handful of fresh basil leaves, slivered

VENETIAN PEPERONATA

"*In Venice they don't bother to peel the peppers or wash the mushrooms,*" *Francesco remarks as he starts to discuss this savory peperonata, a vegetable mélange that can double as a sauce for pasta, an accompaniment for fish, or a topping for polenta. But oddly enough, at the same time, the Venetians do not use the inside of the eggplant for this dish. "The inside of the eggplant makes the mixture too mushy and watery," Francesco explains. It's best to use slender eggplants and scoop out the flesh to within about ½ inch (1.3 cm) of the skin.*

Quarter the eggplant and cut away the flesh to within ½ inch (1.3 cm) of the skin. Save the center of the eggplant for another use—a soup perhaps—and cut the skin in slivers about ¼ inch (6 mm) wide.

Heat the oil in a large, heavy skillet. Add the onion and garlic and sauté over medium heat, stirring, until the onion is golden, about 15 minutes. Add the peppers and sauté another 10 to 15 minutes. Add the eggplant and zucchini and, if needed, more oil. Continue to sauté another 15 to 20 minutes.

Stir in the tomatoes and cook another few minutes, then season with salt and pepper, stir in the basil, and serve. Or set aside and reheat to serve with other ingredients.

MAKES 4 SERVINGS.

INGREDIENTS

3 tablespoons (45 ml) extra virgin olive oil

⅔ cup (80 g) chopped onion

2 cloves garlic, slivered

I pound (500 g) zucchini (courgettes), diced

Salt and freshly ground black pepper to taste

½ tablespoon (8 g) unsalted butter

I tablespoon chopped fresh mint or
    2 tablespoons (15 g) freshly grated
    Parmesan cheese

ZUCCHINI IN UMIDO

*W*ith fresh, flavorful ingredients, the simplest preparations, like this one for stewed zucchini, become irresistibly delectable. Francesco prepared an enormous quantity of this dish for a big outdoor buffet at his cousin's house in Mestre. It was a perfect foil for grilled squid and smoky chunks of grilled baby monkfish tails. It can also be served over penne or fettuccine (recipe on page 73).

Heat the oil in a large, heavy skillet. Add the onion and cook over low heat until it is tender and golden, about 10 minutes. Stir in the garlic, cook another minute, then add the zucchini.

Cook, stirring from time to time, until the zucchini is tender, about 10 minutes longer. Season with salt and pepper and stir in the butter.

To serve with fish, stir in the mint. Or serve as a vegetable topped with freshly grated Parmesan cheese.

MAKES 2 TO 3 SERVINGS.

INGREDIENTS

4 large zucchini (courgettes), each about
 6 ounces (185 g)

2 tablespoons (30 ml) extra virgin olive oil

¼ cup (30 g) finely chopped onion

¼ cup (30 g) finely chopped celery

¼ cup (30 g) finely chopped carrot

4 cloves garlic, minced

2 bay leaves

2 tablespoons minced fresh basil

1 tablespoon fresh rosemary leaves

2 tablespoons (30 ml) dry white wine

STUFFED ZUCCHINI

"*This is a good example of food we do at home, not in the restaurant,*" *Francesco says. The zucchini stuffed with well-seasoned veal are excellent served hot or at room tempera-ture. You might drizzle them with a little basil oil (recipe on page 87) before serving.*

Slice the zucchini in half lengthwise. Scoop out the centers and discard them, leaving shells about ½ inch (1.3 cm) thick.

Heat the oil in a heavy skillet. Add the onion, celery, carrot, garlic, and bay leaves and sauté over low heat until the vegetables are soft but not brown. Remove from the heat, discard the bay leaves, and add the basil, rosemary, and wine. Stir in the veal and grind the mixture together in a meat grinder or food processor.

Add the cheese and egg to the meat mixture and mix to combine. Season with salt and pepper.

1 pound (500 g) boneless veal, in small pieces

1 cup (125 g) freshly grated Parmesan cheese

1 large egg, beaten

Salt and freshly ground black pepper to taste

2 tablespoons (30 g) unsalted butter

INGREDIENTS

2 carrots, peeled and sliced

1 cup (125 g) diced peeled acorn or
    butternut squash

1 cup (85 g) small pieces of cauliflower

2 stalks celery, diced

1 small bulb fennel, diced

9 pearl onions, peeled

1 cup (75 g) 1-inch (2.5-cm) pieces of
    slender asparagus

6 tablespoons (90 ml) extra virgin olive oil

2 small red bell peppers (capsicums), seeded
    and diced

3 large cloves garlic

3 sun-dried tomatoes, finely chopped

1½ cups (375 g) chopped tomatoes (fresh,
    oven-dried, or canned)

4 sprigs fresh thyme

Salt and freshly ground black pepper to taste

Preheat the oven to 375°F (190°C). Pack the meat mixture into each zucchini shell and dot with butter. Place the stuffed zucchini in a baking dish and add water to a depth of ½ inch (1.3 cm). Cover the zucchini with a sheet of foil and bake for 25 to 30 minutes. Serve warm or at room temperature.

MAKES 4 SERVINGS.

VEGETABLE CASSEROLE

"The best way to make these vegetables delicious is to cook them in olive oil," Francesco says. His technique for this spezzatino di verdure is to precook all the vegetables, then combine them with the olive oil and seasonings before serving. Francesco recommends serving this vegetable casserole with roast rack of lamb (recipe on page 134).

Steam or boil the carrots, squash, cauliflower, celery, fennel, and onions together about 10 minutes. Add the asparagus and steam for another 2 minutes. Drain the vegetables, plunge them in a large bowl of ice water, and allow them to chill.

Heat 2 tablespoons (30 ml) of the oil in a large, heavy skillet. Add the peppers, garlic, and sun-dried tomatoes. Sauté until the peppers are tender. Stir in the tomatoes, thyme, and remaining olive oil. Cook for 5 minutes longer.

Just before serving, add the cooked vegetables, cook about 5 minutes, then season with salt and pepper and serve.

MAKES 4 SERVINGS.

S·E·A·F·O·O·D

Nothing defines Venice's cuisine like its seafood. No meal is complete without some sea creatures as the fruitful harvest from the surrounding lagoon and the nearby sea washes onto the plate.

"This city aboundeth with good fish," said Fynes Moryson, an English visitor in the early 17th century, when fish were sold twice daily, not only at the bustling Rialto market but also from stalls in St. Mark's Square.

A few silvery anchovies on a square of polenta or some grilled razor clams, pencil-thin and nestled in their pale shells, whet the appetite today as they did centuries ago. Risotto or pasta may be tossed with the inevitable cuttlefish or squid, dark with ink or not, to be followed by meaty monkfish perhaps, or trout from mountain streams in the Alto Adige. If there were a way to serve fish for dessert, Venetians would do so gladly.

It begins at the Rialto market at water's edge. Boats sidle up to the slick stone dock and unload wicker and wire baskets of glistening black mussels, rough gray oysters, and squirming *canocie*, the sweet mantis shrimp that look like fossilized trilobites. Tiny white snails, ropy piles of eels and octopuses, huge fresh tuna strung on grappling hooks, boxes of small greenish *gò* fish with big eyes, striped *marmore*

fish, silver sardines, sleek spotted sharks, masses of inky cuttlefish and squid, and even the eggs of the cuttlefish are piled on dripping tables at various stalls under Renaissance arches and alongside newer market buildings. "In Venice even ordinary sole and ugly great skate are striped with delicate lilac lights," said Elizabeth David, the great English food writer, "the sardines shine like newly minted silver coins, pink Venetian scampi are fat and fresh, infinitely enticing in the early dawn."

The fish from the lagoon, some harvested wild but increasingly farm-raised as well, are rich in flavor because their diet, like that of the Venetians themselves further up the food chain, consists of so many tasty sea creatures. And yet there is a lightness and delicacy about Venetian seafood. "Venetians love all the small stuff," Francesco remarks, pointing out piles of tightly closed shells and rows of hand-size silver fish as we prowl the market one morning.

But the delicacy also comes from the integrity and simplicity of the preparation. When seafood is so fresh, it requires minimal intervention. A gloss of butter or oil, a splash of lemon, the added crunch of a handful of bread crumbs, some fragrant fresh herbs, are all it takes to glorify these fine raw materials. Raw? One fishmonger quickly opens a few razor clams for us to slurp on the spot. He offers lemon. "No lemon," growls an old crone laden with string bags as she passes this impromptu buffet.

Appreciation of razor clams sums up the difficulty in reproducing Venetian cooking elsewhere. Where else are tiny razor clams harvested, for example? The earthy food of Tuscany, so popular in many countries, depends on ingredients that travel better than those of the Veneto.

But the sensibility of the Venetian table and its cooking can certainly be applied to other places, especially when it comes to handling seafood. All it takes is an uncompromising insistence on freshness. Francesco freely uses salmon, halibut, littleneck clams, lobster, and the like, informing these ingredients with Venetian taste. Venice is the only place, outside some areas in the eastern United States, where soft-shell crabs are routinely gathered and eaten. Called *molecche* in Venetian dialect, they are prized at their tiniest, in April and May, when they are simply floured and fried as they have been since at least the 17th century.

You will not find razor clams in your local fish market. Nor will the classic Venetian scampi, the langoustines of the Adriatic, be available. If you do find fresh scampi in a market, they are likely to have been imported from Iceland and cost a doge's ransom. They will have a harder shell and may be inconsistent in quality. If you are intrigued, then by all means try them. Have them split, then grill them quickly with a brushing of butter and a dusting of fresh herbs.

The recipes crafted by Francesco depend on more readily available varieties. What is most important is the freshness. Therefore, if a particular recipe tempts but the fish of choice appears less than Rialto-fresh, do not hesitate to substitute one fish for another. Mussels can often be used instead of clams (or vice versa), tilefish in place of monkfish, smelts for sardines.

In addition to the seafood recipes in this chapter, there are seafood-based recipes in other chapters:

ANTIPASTO

RICE, POLENTA & PASTA

VEGETABLES

GRILLED MONKFISH WITH RADICCHIO AND POLENTA

INGREDIENTS

1 monkfish tail, about 2 pounds (1 kg)

Juice of 2 lemons

½ cup (125 ml) extra virgin olive oil

4 tablespoons finely chopped mixed fresh herbs (rosemary, thyme, sage)

2 large cloves garlic, finely minced

Salt and freshly ground black pepper to taste

4 cups (1 l) water

1 cup (250 g) white cornmeal for polenta

2 heads radicchio, quartered

Lemon wedges for garnish

Monica Billi, Francesco's cousin who lives near Mestre, the mainland lifeline to Venice, says that they serve monkfish to children because it has no bones. Her favorite preparation is to gloss it with olive oil and chopped herbs, cook it simply on the grill, and accompany it with grilled radicchio and squares of grilled white polenta for a lush panoply of textures, flavors, and colors. This dish can be the centerpiece of an alfresco country lunch for family and friends.

"Whole monkfish tails are good for grilling when they are not too large," Francesco says. "They are thick enough to become attractively brown without overcooking." In Italian monkfish is coda di rospo, or "monkfish tail," the only part of this bottom fish that is eaten.

Trim any gray membrane from the monkfish. Place in a shallow dish and pour the lemon juice, ¼ cup (60 ml) of the olive oil, the chopped herbs, and garlic over it. Season with salt and pepper and allow to marinate for 1 hour.

Meanwhile, bring the water to a simmer and slowly stir in the polenta. Cook, stirring, about 15 minutes. Stir in 2 tablespoons (30 ml) of the olive oil and season with salt and pepper. Spread the polenta in an 8-inch (20-cm) square baking dish and allow it to cool.

Brush the radicchio with the remaining 2 tablespoons (30 ml) olive oil and season with salt and pepper.

Preheat a grill or broiler. Grill the monkfish until it is nicely browned and cooked through, about 25 minutes, turning it to brown evenly. About halfway through the cooking time, place the radicchio on the grill and cook it, turning it as it browns on each side. A few minutes before the fish and radicchio have finished cooking, cut the polenta into 4 squares and place them on the grill to reheat and brown, turning them once to cook on both sides.

Cut the monkfish into thick slices and serve with the radicchio and polenta, garnished with lemon wedges.

MAKES 4 SERVINGS.

ROASTED SARDINES

INGREDIENTS

1 tablespoon extra virgin olive oil

16 whole fresh sardines, cleaned

2 tablespoons minced parsley

4 cloves garlic, minced

2 teaspoons fresh rosemary leaves

2 teaspoons fresh thyme leaves

Salt and freshly ground black pepper to taste

¼ cup (30 g) fine dry bread crumbs

1 tablespoon freshly grated Parmesan cheese

1 lemon, cut in 4 wedges

"*This is a very Venetian dish,*" *Francesco declares.* "*Sardines are fish for the poor. Usually we make this dish in the restaurant for the employees, not the customers.*" *Underappreciated in America, fresh sardines are a staple throughout southern Europe and the Middle East. These small fish, with their rich, oily, and delicious flesh, are served dozens of ways. They may be simply grilled, sautéed and seasoned with a typically Venetian sweet-and-sour marinade, or roasted with a sharp, herbaceous seasoning, the way Francesco likes them best.*

Fresh sardines are often sold in fish markets that cater to an Italian or Greek clientele. And when it comes to sardines, as with other oily fish, sparkling freshness is crucial. If acceptable sardines are unavailable, the recipe also works well with smelts. Francesco says the secret ingredient in the recipe is the bit of Parmesan cheese, which adds a sharpness without actually contributing its flavor.

Preheat the oven to 450°F (230°C). Spread the oil on a baking sheet.

Rinse the sardines and pat them dry. Remove the heads of the sardines by inserting your thumb into the fish where the head joins the body and pushing the head off. Pull out the central bone. Flatten the sardines without separating the 2 fillets and place them, skin side down, on the baking sheet.

Briefly chop 1½ tablespoons of the parsley with the garlic, rosemary, and thyme. Season with salt and pepper. Spread this mixture on the flesh of each sardine. Sprinkle 1 tablespoon of the bread crumbs and the cheese over all the sardines. Close up the sardines, sandwiching the filling inside.

Sprinkle the tops of the sardines with the remaining bread crumbs and parsley.

Place in the oven and bake about 5 minutes. Serve at once with lemon.

MAKES 4 SERVINGS.

RED SNAPPER WITH RED ONION, PIGNOLI, AND RAISINS ("IN SAOR")

INGREDIENTS

1 whole red snapper, about 2 pounds (1 kg),
   boned and split in 2 fillets

4 tablespoons (60 ml) extra virgin olive oil

2 cups (250 g) thinly sliced red onions

2 tablespoons (30 ml) red wine vinegar

1 tablespoon dry red wine

1 teaspoon sugar

1 teaspoon pignoli

1 teaspoon golden raisins

1 teaspoon freshly grated orange zest

Red snapper is not a Venetian fish, but you are unlikely to find sea bream, a variety the Venetians might use for a recipe like this. Besides, like the reveler who dons a fanciful mask and becomes Venetian for Carnevale, red snapper takes on a Venetian accent when it is dressed in a seductively sweet-sour mixture of onions, raisins, and pignoli akin to the classic preparation "in saor." "The important thing is for the fish to be fresh," Francesco cautions. Buy a whole red snapper and have the fish market split and bone it. Black sea bass can be substituted for the red snapper.

Arrange the fillets skin side down on a broiling pan and brush with 1 tablespoon of the olive oil. Preheat a broiler.

Heat 2 tablespoons (30 ml) of the oil in a large, heavy skillet. Add the onions and sauté over medium heat until soft but not brown. Stir in the vinegar and red wine.

Broil the red snapper until lightly browned, about 6 minutes. Do not turn it.

Reheat the onions and mix in the sugar, pignoli, raisins, and orange zest. Stir in the remaining tablespoon of olive oil. Transfer the red snapper to a warm serving dish or 2 warm dinner plates and spoon the onion mixture over it.

MAKES 2 SERVINGS.

I whole salmon fillet, about 2½ pounds
(1.25 kg), with the skin on

½ cup (60 g) peeled, diced fresh horseradish

1½ large green apples (such as Granny
Smith), peeled, cored, and diced

¼ cup (60 ml) white wine vinegar

Salt to taste

⅔ cup (160 ml) extra virgin olive oil

SALMON WITH HORSERADISH SAUCE

*H*orseradish, called cren *in the Alto Adige, is often used in the region around Venice. It's one example of the influence of Austrian cooking in this multicultural region. But in Venice, the ferocious flavor and aroma of freshly grated horseradish is tamed with apple and vinegar—another application of seductive sweet and sour—before being served as a relish with simple sautéed salmon. As for the salmon itself, the care that a chef like Francesco takes in removing the tiny pin bones is a worthwhile bit of extra effort that should become as automatic in the home kitchen as it is in a fine restaurant.*

Run your hand lightly over the salmon, and if you feel any little pin bones sticking up, pull them out with tweezers or small pliers. Cut the salmon into 6 equal portions.

Place the horseradish and apple in a food processor and process until finely grated. Pour in the vinegar through the feed tube, process briefly, then season with salt and set aside with the cover partly ajar to disperse the fumes until ready to serve.

Heat the oil in a heavy skillet. Place the salmon pieces in the skillet, skin side down, and sauté 4 to 6 minutes, until the skin is very crisp but the top ½ inch (1.3 cm) of the fish still looks uncooked. Cover the pan for a minute, uncover, and transfer the fish, skin side up, to 6 warm dinner plates. Spoon some of the horseradish mixture alongside and serve.

MAKES 6 SERVINGS.

HALIBUT WITH BROCCOLI

*B*read crumbs seasoned with fresh herbs are one of Francesco's favorite touches for dressing up a variety of dishes. This handsome dish, with broccoli adorning the fish in its browned crust, could be served with mashed Parmesan potatoes (recipe on page 98).

INGREDIENTS

1 cup (75 g) broccoli florets

¼ cup (15 g) fresh bread crumbs

2 teaspoons minced fresh sage

1½ pounds (750 g) halibut fillets, in 4 equal pieces

½ cup (125 ml) extra virgin olive oil

½ cup (125 ml) fish stock (recipe on page 86)

6 tablespoons (90 ml) fresh lemon juice

Salt and freshly ground black pepper to taste

Steam the broccoli until just tender but still bright green, about 5 minutes. Refresh in cold water, drain, and set aside. Mix the bread crumbs with half the sage and coat the halibut with this mixture.

Heat 3 tablespoons (45 ml) of the oil in a heavy nonstick skillet, add the fish, and sauté about 5 minutes on each side, or longer if the fillets are very thick, until the fish is just cooked through. Remove the fish from the skillet, transfer to a serving dish, and keep warm.

Add the remaining oil, the fish stock, and lemon juice to the skillet. Stir in the broccoli and remaining sage. Cook just long enough to reheat the broccoli, season with salt and pepper, then spoon the broccoli and sauce around the fish and serve.

MAKES 4 SERVINGS.

BROCHETTE OF SWORDFISH

*D*eftly skewering an assortment of ingredients and then searing them on the grill makes for attractive presentation. Francesco alternates colorful vegetables—some raw, some cooked—with fish, and lightly coats them with bread crumbs before grilling. He uses long bamboo skewers that have been soaked in cold water and threads the food on pairs of them, a tip worth remembering. "With two skewers the food will not spin around and is less likely to fall off," he points out. Bamboo skewers are better than metal ones because they do not conduct heat well and will not cause the fish to overcook.

First place 8 long bamboo skewers in cold water to soak.

Finely chop the garlic with the herbs, season with black pepper, mix with the bread crumbs, and set aside.

Remove the stems from the mushrooms. Place the mushroom caps in a small saucepan with the lemon juice and enough water to cover. Bring to a boil, then drain immediately. Set aside. Core and seed the peppers and cut them into 2-inch (5-cm) squares. You should have 16 squares of pepper.

Trim any skin from the swordfish and cut the fish into 12 uniform medallions, about 1½ × 2 inches (4 × 5 cm). Wrap each in ½ strip of the bacon. Peel the roasted garlic cloves. Peel the onion, quarter it, and separate it into layers.

Preheat a grill or broiler. Thread the ingredients, just slightly off center, on each of 4 skewers, starting with a mushroom cap, then a roasted garlic clove, then a chunk of bacon-wrapped swordfish, taking care to put the skewer through the bacon as well as the fish. Follow with a square of red pepper, a piece of onion, another square of pepper, a chunk of swordfish. Continue with pepper, onion, pepper, swordfish, garlic, and mushroom. Insert a second skewer about ½ inch (1.3 cm) from the first in each brochette. Repeat with the remaining skewers.

Lightly season the skewers with salt and pepper, brush with olive oil, and roll in the bread crumb mixture to coat lightly. Grill or broil the skewers 6 to 8 minutes, turning them as they brown.

Makes 4 servings.

INGREDIENTS

1 small clove garlic

1 tablespoon mixed fresh herbs (rosemary, thyme, sage)

Freshly ground black pepper to taste

¾ cup (90 g) dry bread crumbs

8 large white mushrooms

Juice of ½ lemon

2 bell peppers (capsicums), 1 red and 1 yellow or 2 red

1¾ pounds (875 g) swordfish, 1½ inches (4 cm) thick

6 strips bacon

8 large cloves roasted garlic (recipe on page 71)

1 sweet onion, preferably Vidalia

Salt to taste

3 tablespoons (45 ml) extra virgin olive oil

INGREDIENTS

1 3-pound (1.5-kg) black sea bass, cleaned but not scaled

Several sprigs fresh herbs (rosemary, oregano, thyme)

3 cloves garlic, peeled

4 pounds (2 kg) kosher salt or sea salt

1 cup (125 g) flour

½ cup (125 ml) water

6 oven-dried tomatoes (recipe on page 71), chopped

Juice of 1 lemon

¼ cup (60 ml) basil oil (recipe on page 87)

Salt and freshly ground pepper to taste

WHOLE FISH IN SALT CRUST

"For this recipe you need a fish with the scales left on. Otherwise, the salt will penetrate the fish," Francesco says. It is another method of steaming and, properly done, results in impeccably moist and meaty fish that is not at all salty. To be sure of obtaining a fish with the scales on, it is probably necessary to order one in advance from a reliable fishmonger.

Preheat the oven to 400°F (200°C). Trim the fins and tail of the fish with scissors. Stuff the cavity of the fish with the herbs and garlic and sew up the cavity with strong thread or dental floss.

Mix the salt and flour together, then mix in the water to make a thick, fairly dry paste. Line a baking sheet with foil. Spread part of the salt mixture on the foil in a layer somewhat larger than the fish. Place the fish on the salt layer, then completely bury the fish in the remaining salt mixture, packing it on to cover the fish completely.

Place in the oven and bake 45 minutes.

Mix the tomatoes with the lemon juice and basil oil, season with salt and pepper, and set aside.

Lifting the fish and foil together, transfer the fish with the foil to a serving platter. To serve, carefully crack the salt crust and lift off the top layer. Wipe the utensils clean and lift off the skin of the fish. Then serve the exposed flesh, spooning a little of the tomato sauce over each serving. Be careful not to allow any of the salt to get on the flesh of the fish. Lift off the bones and serve the rest of the fish, leaving the skin on the salt.

MAKES 4 SERVINGS.

WHOLE FISH IN PARCHMENT

INGREDIENTS

3 tablespoons (45 ml) extra virgin olive oil

4 large strips orange peel

4 large strips lemon peel

1 3½-pound (1.75-kg) fish (sea bass, striped bass, or red snapper), cleaned

Salt to taste

1 cup (250 g) chopped fresh or oven-dried tomato (recipe on page 71)

1 sprig fresh oregano

1 sprig fresh rosemary

4 cloves garlic, sliced

Pinch of hot red pepper flakes

1 cup (250 ml) fish stock (recipe on page 86)

Juice of 1 orange

Juice of ½ lemon

2 tablespoons slivered fresh basil leaves

Freshly ground black pepper to taste

*C*ooking fish in a parchment wrap is essentially a method of steaming. Francesco urges that the whole fish, not just fillets or steaks, be used. "You need the bones, and it has to be thick so you get all the succulence and flavor," he says. The touch of citrus gives the fish a decidedly Venetian cast.

Preheat the oven to 400°F (200°C). Spread a large sheet of parchment paper, 18 × 36 inches (45 × 90 cm), on a work surface and brush it with 1 tablespoon of the olive oil.

Scatter half the strips of orange and lemon peel on the parchment, then place the fish on them. Season the fish inside and out with salt. Spread 1 tablespoon of the tomato in the cavity of the fish along with the oregano and rosemary. Scatter the remaining peels over the fish along with another 6 tablespoons (90 g) of the tomato, the garlic, and red pepper flakes. Pour the fish stock and orange juice over the fish.

Cover with 2 more sheets of parchment and roll the edges of the top and bottom sheets of parchment paper together to seal them. Staple them together around the edges. Transfer the entire package to a baking sheet, place in the oven, and bake for 45 minutes.

While the fish is baking, mix the remaining tomato with the lemon juice, remaining olive oil, and basil leaves. Season with salt and pepper and set aside.

When the fish is done, carefully transfer the parchment package to a large platter. To serve, cut around the edges with scissors and lift off the top layer of parchment. Lift off the skin of the fish, then serve portions of the fish, lifting the top layer off the bones. Remove the large central bones, then serve the bottom layer of the fish. Spoon the juices contained in the parchment and some of the tomato-lemon-oil mixture on each serving.

MAKES 4 SERVINGS.

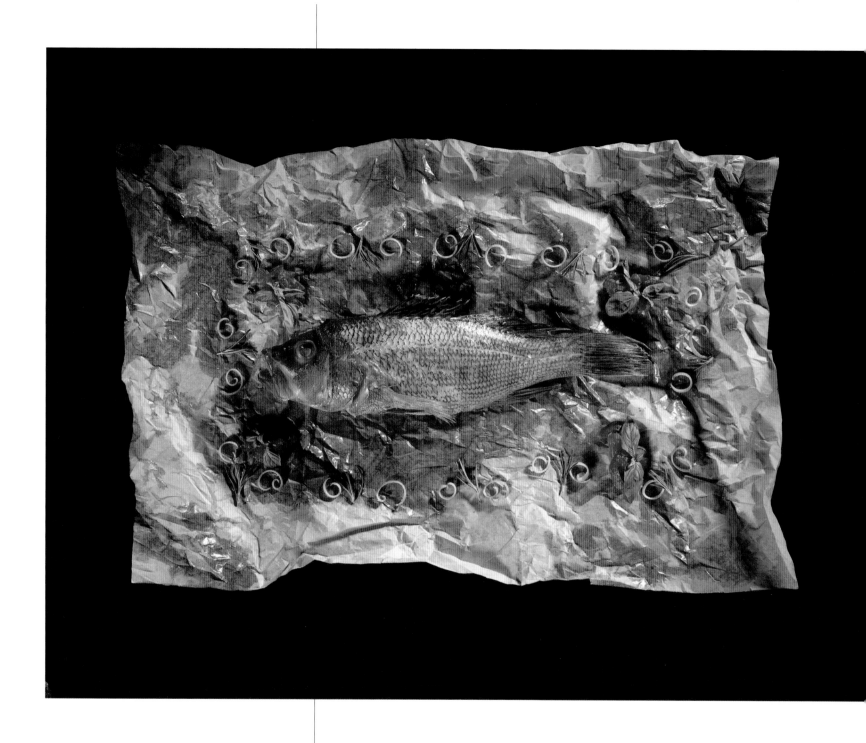

FRIED CALAMARI

"*It's nice to serve fried calamari on a sheet of parchment paper,*" Francesco says. *The paper not only adds an inviting note of informality but also helps absorb any excess oil from the crisp fried rings of squid. And for Francesco, it adds a Proustian touch. "When I was a kid and went to the market with my mother, I was always fascinated by the way the butcher or the fisherman would wrap something up in the paper and hand it to my mother, saying, '200 lire, signora.' Today the crumple of parchment paper always brings back these memories."*

If using whole squid, clean them by removing the interior cartilage. Slice the cleaned squid in rings.

Mix the flour and paprika together in a large bowl. Begin heating the oil to a depth of 2 inches (5 cm) in a large saucepan or a wok.

Place the squid rings and tentacles in the flour and toss to coat them. When the oil is hot, add the squid rings, separating them and shaking off as much excess flour as possible. Fry them until they are light gold, then drain on absorbent paper. Continue frying the squid until they are all done. Then quickly fry the sage leaves and parsley.

Dust the squid with salt and pile onto a large sheet of parchment paper in a bowl or a basket. Garnish with the fried herbs and serve with lemon wedges.

MAKES 4 TO 6 SERVINGS.

INGREDIENTS

2 pounds (1 kg) whole medium-size to small
  squid (about 1¼ pounds/625 g), cleaned

2½ cups (310 g) flour

1 tablespoon paprika

Corn oil for deep frying

Leaves from 2 large sprigs fresh sage

4 tablespoons curly parsley leaves

Salt to taste

Lemon wedges

SHRIMP WITH ARTICHOKES

Gabriella Mariotti, a Venetian who lives most of the time in New York, calls this dish of shrimp with artichokes and a whiff of curry scampi e carciofi alla veneziana. When she is in Venice, she uses scampi. "You cannot get them in New York so I buy jumbo shrimp instead," she says. And if the small artichokes she prefers are not available, large ones, trimmed down to the fleshy heart, can be used instead. This is a savory, slightly exotic, and flavorful preparation, quickly made to serve as a first course or a main dish.

If the artichokes are small, trim the stems to within ½ inch (1.3 cm) of the bases and remove the tougher outer leaves. Cut each artichoke in eighths and place in a bowl. Toss with the lemon juice and cover with water. Set aside for 15 minutes. If you are using medium-size artichokes, trim the stems flush with the bases and remove all the leaves. Using a sharp knife, cut away the center choke, leaving just the fleshy bottom, or heart, of each artichoke. Cut each into eighths and treat with the lemon as previously described.

Drain the artichoke pieces.

Heat half the oil in a heavy skillet over medium heat. Add the artichokes, parsley, and garlic, reduce the heat to low, and cook, stirring from time to time, about 20 minutes, until the artichokes are lightly browned and tender when pierced with a sharp knife.

While the artichokes are cooking, dissolve the curry powder in 1 tablespoon of the wine.

When the artichokes are tender, remove them from the skillet and set aside. Season the flour with salt and pepper and toss the shrimp in the flour to coat them lightly. Add the remaining oil to the skillet and increase the heat to medium.

Add the shrimp to the skillet and stir-fry a minute or two, until they turn pink. Pour in the curry powder mixture, stir, then add the remaining wine. Cook, stirring, until the wine just films the bottom of the pan. Return the artichokes to the pan, stir, season with salt and pepper, and serve.

MAKES 4 SERVINGS AS AN APPETIZER, 2 TO 3 SERVINGS AS A MAIN DISH.

INGREDIENTS

6 small or 4 medium-size artichokes

Juice of 1 lemon

3 tablespoons (45 ml) extra virgin olive oil

1 tablespoon flat-leaf (Italian) parsley

1 large clove garlic, chopped

1 teaspoon curry powder

½ cup (125 ml) dry white wine

2 tablespoons flour

Salt and freshly ground black pepper to taste

12 jumbo shrimp (prawns), peeled and deveined

INGREDIENTS

1 cup (185 g) dried borlotti (cranberry)
  beans or pinto beans

1 small carrot, peeled

1 small onion, peeled

½ stalk celery

2 cloves garlic, peeled

Small sprigs fresh rosemary, thyme, and
  flat-leaf (Italian) parsley tied together

¼ cup (60 ml) extra virgin olive oil

Salt and freshly ground black pepper to taste

10 large sea scallops

3 tablespoons (22 g) dry bread crumbs

1½ tablespoons freshly grated Parmesan cheese

½ teaspoon finely minced flat-leaf (Italian)
  parsley

½ teaspoon finely minced fresh thyme

Sprigs fresh thyme for garnish

SEA SCALLOPS WITH BEAN CREAM

In Tuscany the white bean (cannellini) is king, but Venice prefers the variegated pinto or borlotti bean. "We never even saw white beans in Venice when I was growing up," Francesco says. In this dish a purée of the beans becomes the velvety, herb-infused sauce for meaty seared sea scallops.

Cover the beans with water to a depth of 1 inch (2.5 cm) and allow to soak 4 hours or overnight. Drain the beans, place them in a saucepan, and cover with water to a depth of 1 inch (2.5 cm). Add the carrot, onion, celery, garlic, and bunch of herbs. Bring to a simmer and cook, partly covered, until the beans are tender, about 45 minutes to 1 hour. In the beginning of the cooking, you may have to skim foam that collects on the surface. When the beans are tender, drain them, reserving ½ cup (125 ml) of the cooking liquid.

Purée all but 1 cup (250 g) of the beans in a food processor with the cooked garlic, carrot, onion, and reserved cooking liquid. Add 2 tablespoons (30 ml) of the olive oil and season with salt and pepper. Transfer to a saucepan and set aside.

Slice the sea scallops in half horizontally. Mix the bread crumbs with the cheese, parsley, and thyme and season with salt and pepper. Dust the sea scallops with the bread crumb mixture.

Heat the remaining oil in a heavy skillet. Lightly brown the slices of sea scallops in the oil, then transfer them to absorbent paper. Toss the reserved cup of beans in the skillet just enough to reheat them. Reheat the bean sauce.

To serve, spoon 5 to 6 tablespoons (75 to 90 ml) of the bean sauce on each of 4 warm plates. Arrange 5 slices of the scallops, slightly overlapping, in a circle on the sauce. Spoon a few tablespoons of the whole beans in the center, garnish with sprigs of thyme, and serve.

Photograph on page 104.

Makes 4 servings.

INGREDIENTS

5 tablespoons (75 ml) extra virgin olive oil

12 mussels

1 pound (500 g) cockles, Manila clams, or
littleneck clams

4 to 5 cups (1 to 1.25 l) fish stock
(recipe on page 86)

¼ bulb fresh fennel, sliced

4 small carrots, peeled

1 cup (250 ml) dry white wine

1 pound (500 g) jumbo shrimp (prawns),
shelled

12 ounces (375 g) salmon fillet, in 3-inch
(7.5-cm) chunks

12 ounces (375 g) sea bass fillet, in 3-inch
(7.5-cm) chunks

1 bunch scallions (spring onions), trimmed to
3-inch (7.5-cm) lengths

Salt and freshly ground white pepper to taste

4 cups (1 kg) cooked borlotti (cranberry)
beans (recipe on page 57, paragraphs 1
and 2)

VENETIAN SEAFOOD STEW

"*Seafood stews are not easy to make because you really have to cook each kind of fish separately so that nothing is overcooked,*" Francesco advises. The end result is fresh, light, and simple. Some tiny red potatoes, like the ones that beckon invitingly from baskets in Venice's Rialto market, could be simply steamed, dusted with fresh rosemary, drizzled with olive oil, and served alongside the seafood stew, to be added to each dish at the table.

Heat 2 tablespoons (30 ml) of the oil in a heavy 4- to 5-quart (4- to 5-l) saucepan or shallow casserole. Add the mussels and cockles or clams, cover, and steam over medium heat until they open, about 10 minutes. Remove the mussels and cockles from the pan with a slotted spoon, place in a bowl, and cover.

Add 4 cups (1 l) of the fish stock and the fennel, carrots, and wine to the saucepan, bring to a simmer, and add the shrimp. Cook about a minute, until the shrimp turn pink, then remove them with a slotted spoon. Place in a dish and cover.

Add the salmon and bass to the pan, cook about 2 minutes, turn the pieces of fish, then return the shrimp, mussels, and cockles to the pan. Add the scallions and season the stock with salt and pepper. Add the beans, bring to a simmer, and, if necessary, add the additional stock. Stir in the remaining olive oil and serve in shallow bowls.

MAKES 6 SERVINGS.

P·O·U·L·T·R·Y, M·E·A·T & G·A·M·E

Meat does not whet the Venetian appetite. During the 16th century, when meat was served at banquets, it was preceded and followed by "crabs and oysters, partridges, peacocks and guinea fowl, pigeons and pheasants," reported one English observer. In the early 17th century, Henry Wotten, the ambassador from England, wrote in his diaries about shooting ducks in the lagoon, "a pretty sport of killing them on the wing," something not yet done in England.

Ducks and other small birds, chicken, and rabbit revolving on a spit and served with steaming polenta are more tempting in this waterbound city than portions of red meat and large game. Until 1873, when the market stalls blighting St. Mark's Square were torn down, the square would be filled with chicken coops every morning.

Although meat is not an important component of the relatively frugal Venetian menu, ironically, one of the area's most famous dishes, *fegato alla veneziana*, liver and onions, is made with rich meat. Adam Tihany likes to point out the similarity between this dish, in which strips of liver are sautéed with a profusion of golden onions, and the Chinese stir-fry. Whether this represents a genuine Marco Polo connection or a fantasy is immaterial. It is the ultimate in liver and onions.

Sausages and innards are important components of the menu, especially in the colder mountain areas north of the city, the only area of the region that dotes on the pig.

The Venetian love of spices is evident in many of the dishes made with poultry, game, and meat. And the herbed salt that Francesco uses for preparing poultry and meats is as Venetian as any recipe in this chapter. Venetian commerce was founded on the city's control of the salt produced along its sea coast and its ability to trade this precious commodity inland and in other countries.

There are recipes using meat, game, and poultry in other chapters:

ANTIPASTO

Black Peppered Beef Carpaccio with Tarragon Dressing, page 46
Country Terrine, page 49

RICE, POLENTA & PASTA

Bigoli with Duck and Radicchio, page 79

VEGETABLES

Stuffed Zucchini, page 102

ROAST CHICKEN WITH HERBED SALT

INGREDIENTS

1 roasting chicken, about 5 pounds (2.5 kg)

2 tablespoons (30 g) herbed salt (recipe on page 136)

3 large cloves garlic

3 sprigs fresh rosemary

2 sprigs fresh thyme

"*My first job in New York was grilling chickens at DDL Food Show, the big fancy food store that Dino di Laurentiis, the movie director, opened on Columbus Avenue in 1983,*" Francesco recalls. "*At most I had call for 3 or 4 chickens a day, but when Dino asked how many chickens I was cooking, I told him 90 to 100 because I was afraid to lose my job.*" *Francesco's own roast chicken could not be simpler. The secret ingredient is the herbed salt he uses as seasoning.*

Preheat the oven to 400°F (200°C). Truss the chicken and rub it inside and out with the herbed salt. Tuck the cloves of garlic and sprigs of rosemary and thyme inside the chicken.

Guinea Hen with Black Pepper Sauce

Place the chicken on a rack and roast until golden brown, about 1½ hours. Remove from the oven and let stand at room temperature at least 15 minutes before disjointing or carving.

Serve with pan juices.

Photograph on page 122.

Photograph on page 122.

MAKES 4 SERVINGS.

GUINEA HEN WITH BLACK PEPPER SAUCE

In Venice both rich and poor hunted birds for sport and sustenance. This recipe for guinea hen with black pepper sauce suggests the Renaissance, when spice played an important role in flavoring, often counterbalanced with a touch of sweetness. "Game birds are lean," Francesco says, "which is why we use the bacon." Baby pheasant can be substituted.

INGREDIENTS

2 large sprigs fresh rosemary

2 cloves garlic, halved

1 2½-pound (1.25-kg) guinea hen or baby pheasant

1 teaspoon herbed salt (recipe on page 136)

3 tablespoons (45 ml) extra virgin olive oil

2 ounces (60 g) slab bacon, cut in chunks

1 carrot, cut in chunks

1 stalk celery, cut in chunks

1 onion, cut in chunks

½ cup (125 ml) dry white wine

3 tablespoons (45 ml) vegetable stock (recipe on page 85)

4 teaspoons whole black peppercorns

¼ teaspoon crushed black peppercorns

Salt to taste

Place the rosemary and garlic in the cavity of the guinea hen. Rub the bird inside and out with the herbed salt, then truss it.

Heat the olive oil in a deep casserole large enough to hold the bird. Sear the bird in the oil on top of the stove to brown it lightly on all sides. Remove the bird from the pan and scatter the slab bacon, carrot, celery, and onion in the casserole.

Preheat the oven to 425°F (220°C). Place the bird on the vegetables in the casserole. Sprinkle the wine and stock around it and scatter 3 teaspoons of the peppercorns in the casserole. Cover the casserole and place in the oven. Roast for 45 minutes.

Remove the guinea hen from the casserole and strain the pan juices into a saucepan. Heat the sauce and add the remaining whole peppercorns and crushed peppercorns. Season to taste with salt. You should have about 1½ cups (375 ml) of sauce.

Remove the trussing from the guinea hen and quarter it. Arrange it on a platter with the vegetables and serve with the sauce alongside.

MAKES 4 SERVINGS.

CHICKEN STUFFED WITH PROSCIUTTO AND FONTINA

INGREDIENTS

1 whole skinless, boneless chicken breast

4 ounces (125 g) imported Italian fontina
cheese, in 1 piece

2 slices imported prosciutto

2 to 3 tablespoons (30 to 45 g) unsalted butter

6 ounces (185 g) shiitake mushrooms,
stems removed

½ cup (125 ml) dry white wine

3 sprigs fresh rosemary

Salt and freshly ground black pepper to taste

Leaves from 1 bunch arugula (rocket)
(optional)

1 tablespoon extra virgin olive oil (optional)

1 pound (500 g) fresh fettuccine (optional)

"*This is about as fancy as chicken gets in Venice,*" Francesco says. *Chicken with cheese and prosciutto is a northern Italian combination of long standing, the ham and cheese infusing the mild chicken with flavor. Francesco combines the pinwheel slices with mushrooms to serve either on a bed of greens or on pasta. This recipe can be expanded, using as many chicken breasts as needed, to make a buffet party dish. It's convenient because some of the preparation is easily done in advance. Once the chicken is cooked, the slices of stuffed chicken rolls can be arranged around the edge of a platter of arugula salad or cooked pasta.*

Divide the chicken breast into 2 halves. Place each between sheets of waxed paper and pound them thin with a mallet, the flat of a large knife, or a rolling pin.

Trim the rind from the cheese and cut it into 2 thick sticks. Wrap each stick with a slice of prosciutto and place in the center of each flattened chicken breast. Wrap the chicken breast around the prosciutto and cheese to make a sausage shape, then wrap this tightly in plastic and refrigerate for at least 1 hour. It can be refrigerated overnight if that is more convenient.

Heat 2 tablespoons of the butter in a heavy skillet. Quickly brown the chicken rolls over medium-high heat, reduce the heat to low, and scatter the mushrooms in the pan. Sprinkle the wine and rosemary in the pan. Cook, turning the chicken rolls frequently, 15 to 20 minutes. When the first bit of cheese begins to seep out, the chicken is done. Remove it from the pan to a cutting board at once.

Cut each of the rolls at an angle into 6 slices. Cover to keep warm.

Reheat the pan juices and season them to taste with salt and pepper.

To serve, arrange the chicken and mushrooms on a bed of arugula leaves tossed with olive oil and seasoned with salt and pepper. Warm the pan juices and strain them over the chicken. Or serve the chicken and mushrooms on a bed of fettuccine that has been boiled in salted water for 3 minutes and tossed with the remaining tablespoon of butter and the reserved pan juices.

MAKES 4 SERVINGS.

Chicken Stuffed with Prosciutto and Fontina

INGREDIENTS

¼ cup (60 ml) extra virgin olive oil

1 onion, finely chopped

1 carrot, finely chopped

1 stalk celery, finely chopped

4 pigeons (squabs), split

Salt and freshly ground black pepper to taste

Sprigs fresh rosemary

SAUTÉED PIGEON

"*Ernest Hemingway was supposed to have said that when it came to hunting game, Kenya was best, but for birds, Venice.*" *Francesco says it is logical.* "*With so many fish there had to be birds.*"

Heat the oil in a large, heavy skillet. Add the onion, carrot, and celery and sauté until tender but not brown.

Add the squab to the pan and sauté over medium heat until browned on the outside. The breast meat should still be pink inside. Season with salt and pepper.

Serve garnished with rosemary.

MAKES 4 SERVINGS.

PIGEON SOUP WITH BREAD (SOPA COADA)

4 sautéed pigeons (recipe on page 127)

6 cups well-flavored veal, beef, or duck consommé (recipe on page 137)

9 thin slices firm-textured white bread (approximately)

1 tablespoon fresh rosemary leaves

4 tablespoons (30 g) freshly grated Parmesan cheese, plus extra cheese for the table

*H*ere is hearty peasant fare from Treviso and the mountains north of Venice. "Dishes for the poor take longer to cook," Francesco observes. The pigeon soup enriched with bread is a second-day bonus using leftovers or extra pigeons (or ducks, for that matter) that have been sautéed or roasted. "This is traditional food, not something we would serve in a restaurant," Francesco says. Yet the result, a dramatic puff of bread layered with game, consommé, and cheese, is as magnificent as it is delicious.

Remove the meat from the pigeons, chop it, and set aside.

Place the pigeon bones in a saucepan, add the consommé, and simmer 10 minutes. Remove from the heat and strain, discarding the bones.

Line the bottom of a deep 3½- to 4-quart (3.5- to 4-l) casserole with a layer of the bread. Scatter half the chopped pigeon over the bread and sprinkle with half the rosemary and 1 tablespoon of the cheese. Cover with another layer of the bread, then with the rest of the pigeon, the remaining rosemary, and another tablespoon of the cheese. Cover with the remaining bread.

Pour about 4 cups (1 l) of the consommé over the casserole, adding just enough so the consommé comes to the level of the top layer of bread. Sprinkle with another tablespoon of the cheese.

Preheat the oven to 400°F (200°C). Cover the casserole with a sheet of foil, place in the oven, and bake for 1½ hours. Add a little of the remaining consommé to the casserole if it begins to look dry.

Uncover the casserole and sprinkle with the remaining tablespoon of cheese. Bake, uncovered, about 30 minutes longer, until the bread is puffed and browned.

Reheat the remaining consommé.

Ladle the *sopa coada* directly from the casserole into shallow bowls, serving each guest a small cup of hot consommé on the side that can be used to sip alongside or to moisten the *sopa coada* at the table. Pass Parmesan cheese at the table.

MAKES 4 SERVINGS.

PAN-ROASTED QUAIL

INGREDIENTS

4 quail

4 thin slices pancetta

4 fresh sage leaves

1 tablespoon unsalted butter

1 tablespoon vegetable oil

Salt and freshly ground black pepper to taste

¼ cup (60 ml) dry white wine

*T*his is Marcella Hazan's recipe. She prepared it for lunch on the terrace outside the lovely, antique-filled top-floor apartment she and her husband, Victor, share in the Cannaregio district of Venice. The Hazans served the quail with polenta.

Wash the quail thoroughly inside and out under cold running water, then set aside to drain in a colander for 20 minutes. Pat the quail dry and stuff each with a slice of pancetta and a sage leaf.

Place the butter and oil in a heavy sauté pan and place over high heat. Brown the quail on all sides, then sprinkle with salt and pepper and add the wine, turning the birds in it once.

Cook for about 1 minute, then lower the heat to medium and cover the pan, leaving the lid slightly askew. Cook for 45 minutes to 1 hour, until the quail feel tender when probed with a fork and the meat comes away easily from the bone. Check to see if there is sufficient liquid in the pan to keep the quail from sticking. Add a little water if there is not.

Remove the quail from the pan and place on a serving dish. Add 3 tablespoons (45 ml) of water to the pan, increase the heat to high, and cook, loosening the particles clinging to the bottom of the pan with a wooden spoon. If necessary, season the pan juices with salt and pepper, then pour over the quail and serve.

MAKES 2 SERVINGS.

SAUTÉED RABBIT WITH HERBS

INGREDIENTS

2 rabbits, cut in serving pieces

4 sprigs fresh rosemary

4 sprigs fresh thyme

4 sprigs fresh sage

6 cloves garlic, crushed

4 tablespoons (60 ml) extra virgin olive oil

¼ cup (30 g) finely chopped carrot

⅓ cup (40 g) finely chopped celery

½ cup (60 g) finely chopped onion

I cup (250 g) crushed, well-drained fresh or
    canned plum (egg) tomatoes

1½ cups (375 ml) dry white wine

Salt and freshly ground black pepper to taste

½ cup (125 ml) water (approximately)

2 cups (250 g) small white mushrooms

I teaspoon finely chopped fresh rosemary

I teaspoon finely chopped flat-leaf
    (Italian) parsley

I teaspoon finely chopped fresh thyme

"*Rabbit is the new thing in America,*" Francesco says. "*Everybody loves it.*" He explains that in Venice the rabbit would be floured and sautéed because the flour gives a nice brown color and crispy outside. Now, however, the trend toward lighter food has him eliminating the flour and marinating the rabbit first with herbs, garlic, and olive oil for flavor. In this recipe Francesco places a layer of foil or parchment paper directly on the ingredients before putting the pan in the oven. He says it helps concentrate the flavors while allowing excess liquid to evaporate. It's one of many professional kitchen techniques worth remembering at home.

Place the rabbit pieces in a large bowl and toss with the sprigs of rosemary, thyme, and sage, 2 cloves of the garlic, and 3 tablespoons (45 ml) of the oil. Set aside to marinate for 4 hours.

In a large sauté pan, heat ½ tablespoon of the remaining oil, add the rabbit pieces, and sauté over high heat until they are lightly browned. Remove them from the pan.

Add the carrot, celery, onion, and remaining garlic to the pan. Sauté until the vegetables are tender. Add the tomatoes to the pan, then stir in the wine. Bring to a simmer, return the rabbit pieces to the pan, and season with salt and pepper. Add a little water if necessary, so that the rabbit is barely covered with the sauce.

Preheat the oven to 350°F (180°C). Place a piece of foil directly on the surface of the ingredients, place the pan in the oven, and bake for 2 hours. Add a little more water if necessary.

While the rabbit is baking, sauté the mushrooms over high heat in the remaining ½ tablespoon of oil. After the rabbit has baked for 1½ hours, add the sautéed mushrooms to the pan.

When the rabbit is done, check the seasonings. Add the chopped herbs and serve.

MAKES 6 TO 8 SERVINGS.

FEGATO ALLA VENEZIANA

"I love this dish the way it's done in Venice, with the liver in small pieces," Francesco says. "But when Americans come into Remi, they want the liver medium-rare and that's impossible, so I started making it with big pieces of liver." This is another of those dishes that Adam Tihany cites as evidence of the Chinese connection. It's simply a stir-fry. Another theory connects the small pieces of meat to the fork, a utensil first used at the table in Venice. Fynes Moryson, the early-17th-century visitor from England, marveled that Venetians "do not touch their meat; they are served small pieces to be taken up with the fork." The liver in small pieces, with golden onions, is one of the most superb dishes on the menu of the Hotel Cipriani.

1½ tablespoons extra virgin olive oil

2 large sweet onions, sliced thin

3 bay leaves

Salt and freshly ground black pepper to taste

½ cup (125 ml) water

12 ounces (375 g) calves liver, in ½-inch
   (1.3-cm) slices

3 tablespoons (22 g) flour

3 tablespoons (45 ml) white wine vinegar

4 servings white polenta (recipe on page 68)

INGREDIENTS

1½ pounds (750 g) calves tongue

8 large green olives, with pits

2 tablespoons (30 ml) fresh lemon juice

1½ teaspoons anchovy paste (essence)

1½ tablespoons dry bread crumbs

½ cup (125 ml) extra virgin olive oil

2 tablespoons chopped flat-leaf
   (Italian) parsley

Heat the oil in a large, heavy skillet. Add the onions and bay leaves and cook over medium-low heat until the onions are golden. Season with salt and pepper and add the water. Remove from the heat. Transfer the onions to another dish, draining as much oil as possible back into the pan, and set aside.

Lightly dust the pieces of liver with the flour. Heat the oil remaining in the skillet to medium-high. Add the pieces of liver and stir-fry until they are seared.

Return the onions to the skillet, remove the bay leaves, and reheat the onions and liver together. Stir in the vinegar, season with salt and pepper, and serve with white polenta on the side.

MAKES 4 SERVINGS.

TONGUE WITH OLIVE SAUCE

"I can remember how we used to eat all the parts of the animal that nobody else wanted," Francesco says. *"Poor women would go to the butcher and ask for two pounds of lungs for the cat. They did not want to look cheap. But then they'd take it home, flour and fry it, and serve it for dinner." It's no wonder that a liver dish is considered a Venetian classic or that this deliciously savory tongue dish is also popular. The sauce is similar to a green sauce.*

Place the tongue in a saucepan, cover with water, and simmer it about 1 hour. Remove from the water, allow it to cool until it can be handled easily, then remove the skin with a sharp knife. Wrap the tongue in foil or a cloth and set it aside.

Pit the olives and chop them fine. They can be chopped in a food processor, but the texture will be better if they are chopped by hand.

Mix the olives with the lemon juice, anchovy paste, and bread crumbs, then gradually beat in the oil. Fold in the parsley.

Slice the tongue thin and serve it at room temperature with the sauce on the side.

MAKES 4 TO 6 SERVINGS.

ROAST RACKS OF LAMB

Simply roasted racks of lamb are an excellent foil for many of the potato and vegetable dishes typical of Venice. Francesco recommends spezzatino di verdure, *or vegetable casserole, with the racks of lamb. His mashed potatoes are excellent as well.*

INGREDIENTS

2 racks of lamb, Frenched (ask butcher to do this)

2 tablespoons herbed salt (recipe on page 136)

1 teaspoon freshly ground black pepper

Vegetable casserole (recipe on page 103)

Mashed Parmesan potatoes made with 3 potatoes (recipe on page 98)

Preheat the oven to 400°F (200°C). Sear the racks of lamb over high heat in a heavy skillet. Mix the herbed salt and pepper together and use to season the lamb.

Place the racks of lamb, bone sides up, in the skillet or in a roasting pan and bake for about 30 minutes for medium-rare.

Transfer the lamb from the roasting pan to a platter and let stand at room temperature for 10 to 15 minutes. Carve into chops and serve.

Serve with vegetable casserole and mashed potatoes.

MAKES 4 SERVINGS.

PASTISSADA

*P*astissada *is a traditional marinated pot roast that Francesco says at one time was made with horsemeat. Beef is called for now. The best cut to use for succulent results is boneless chuck (or shoulder) filet. Bottom round or rump can be substituted, but the meat will have less flavor and not be quite as moist.*

INGREDIENTS

3 pounds (1.5 kg) beef pot roast (rolled roast), chuck filet, or rump or bottom round

1½ cups (375 ml) dry red wine

½ cup (60 g) chopped onion

½ cup (60 g) chopped carrot

3 tablespoons (45 ml) extra virgin olive oil

1 onion, sliced

Salt and freshly ground black pepper to taste

Soft polenta (recipe on page 68)

Tie the meat at 1½-inch (4-cm) intervals with butcher's cord (or have the butcher do this). Place the meat in a deep bowl and add the wine, chopped onion, and carrot. Cover and refrigerate for 24 hours to marinate, turning once or twice.

Drain the meat and strain the wine marinade. Preheat the oven to 350°F (180°C).

Heat the oil in a heavy saucepan large enough to hold the meat. Add the meat to the pan and brown it on all sides. Pour the strained marinade over the meat, scatter the onion slices in the pan, cover tightly, and place in the oven. Bake for 1½ to 2 hours, until the meat is tender when pierced with a sharp fork.

Allow to cool, then cover and refrigerate overnight in the cooking liquid.

To serve, slice the meat and place in a saucepan or a deep skillet. Pour the sauce over the meat and simmer for 30 minutes, adding more water if there is not enough sauce or if it is becoming too thick. Season with salt and pepper and serve with polenta.

MAKES 6 TO 8 SERVINGS.

HERBED SALT

INGREDIENTS

2 tablespoons chopped fresh rosemary leaves

2 teaspoons fresh thyme leaves

1 tablespoon fresh oregano leaves

6 cloves garlic

1 cup (250 g) salt

"*This is a seasoning we keep on hand in Venice,*" Francesco says. *It's superior to commercial seasoned salt. At one time, Venice had a monopoly on the salt trade in part of Europe.*

Mix all the ingredients together on a large cutting board. With a sharp knife, chop them together until they are uniformly fine.

Transfer the herbed salt to a bowl and leave at room temperature for 24 hours to allow it to dry out. Transfer to a jar, close it tightly, and store in the pantry until ready to use.

MAKES ABOUT 2 CUPS (500 G).

BASIC CONSOMMÉ

INGREDIENTS

3 pounds (1.5 kg) beef and veal bones, preferably with marrow and some meat

1 large onion, quartered

1 carrot

1 stalk celery

12 cups (3 l) cold water

Salt and freshly ground black pepper to taste

"*Real consommé is made with bones,*" Francesco says. He boils the bones in water first, to clean them. Then, he says, it is important to start them in cold water for the consommé so they will release their flavorful juices.

Place the bones in a large saucepan, cover with water, bring to a boil, and boil for 5 minutes. Drain and rinse the bones.

Put the bones in a large, clean stockpot and add the onion, carrot, celery, and cold water. Bring to a simmer and cook gently, skimming the surface from time to time, for 2 hours.

Strain the consommé through a very fine strainer or a strainer lined with a cotton cloth and season with salt and pepper.

MAKES ABOUT 6 CUPS.

Watermelon Granita, recipe on page 141

S·W·E·E·T·S

The Venice of pink palaces and gilded, twisted columns looks like a city made of spun sugar. It was sugar, at one time, that contributed to the city's fortune. Venice had a monopoly not only on salt but also on sugar after Venetian traders gave Europe its first taste of the sweetener from India.

For centuries Venice was the center of sugar refining. The Venetians applied the glassblower's art to sugar and eventually introduced elaborate sugar work to France. A collation served in the doge's palace during the Renaissance for Beatrice d'Este, from the famous family in Ferrara, included at least 300 fanciful items made of gilded sugar.

Sweets, often served as snacks rather than dessert, tempt Venetians and visitors at every turn. The city is filled with pastry shops, their windows laden with fanciful cookies and dessert confections. In the 18th century biscuits, sweets, wine, and lemonade were sold on the street, while in shops called *pestrini* customers ate wafers filled with whipped cream, something of a precursor to the ice cream sandwich. Today a rainbow array of candies and marzipan, glacé fruits, and sugared nuts are sold in confectionary shops and by street vendors.

One of the most popular Italian desserts, tirami-su, consisting of layers of liqueur-soaked cake and rich custard, is a relatively recent Venetian creation, one based on the simple warm, eggy froth of zabaglione. Gossamer cheesecakes, rich tarts paved with a mosaic of fruits, and even, as a legacy of nearby Austria, flaky strudels bursting with apples or cherries tempt the Venetian sweet tooth.

Fragrant seasonal fruits—from springtime's strawberries and cherries, blushing peaches (including the famous white peaches), tender apricots, and lush figs to autumn's juicy grapes, apples, pears, and pomegranates—find their way into Venice's sweets. "Venice offered a wonderful plenty of delicious fruit, of grapes, pears, apples, plums, apricots, and figs most excellent of three or four sorts," reported Thomas Coryat, who visited the city from England in the early 17th century. By that time the fruits brought to the marketplace for sale came from towns under Venice's domain.

These fruits may be the inspiration for the gelato, sorbetto, and granita makers whose confections brighten the afternoon or late evening. In 1755 at a banquet for 180 people in the Palazzo Nani, a special course of fruit ices was served on 32 silver salvers. Today coffee at historic Florian on St. Mark's Square often means coffee and gelato, just as it has for hundreds of years. Marcel Proust ate granita there, which he described as "honeycombed ice."

Fruits are often dried or preserved in sugar and can be found as such in a host of confections. Cornmeal may give intriguing texture to a cookie or brioche. Rosewater and lavender, candied flower petals, and citrus peels may add a touch of the baroque. And spices like saffron, ginger, cinnamon, cloves, and nutmeg, for which Venetian traders were famous, may also find their way into desserts, providing a whiff of the exotic East and testifying to Venice's love of richness and luxury.

The finish to a meal—or an afternoon snack, for that matter—invariably includes *golosezi*, an assortment of fanciful cookies, nut brittles, candied fruit, and chocolate truffles, providing small, sweet mouthfuls that linger, so that the dinner and the taste of Venice last.

SWEETS

ESPRESSO GRANITA

INGREDIENTS

2½ cups (625 ml) warm brewed
   espresso coffee

⅓ cup (90 g) superfine (caster) sugar

2 teaspoons sambuca liqueur

Whipped cream (optional)

Frozen espresso granita, an intense slush, is a welcoming restorative on a steamy day. It's important to start with top-quality brewed espresso at its most intense.

Combine the espresso and sugar, stirring until the sugar dissolves. Stir in the liqueur.

Chill the mixture in the refrigerator for 1 hour, then transfer it to a metal bowl and place it in the freezer. Every 30 minutes, whip the mixture, using a manual or electric beater. Continue freezing and beating the mixture until it is uniformly slushy, about 2 hours. Freeze another hour before serving.

Spoon the granita into goblets and, if desired, serve topped with whipped cream.

MAKES 6 SERVINGS.

WATERMELON GRANITA

INGREDIENTS

3 cups (450 g) cubed seedless watermelon

5 tablespoons (75 ml) fresh lemon juice

⅔ cup (155 g) superfine (caster) sugar
   (approximately)

A café overlooking the Grand Canal or St. Mark's Square on a warm summer afternoon begs for a cool confection. An icy watermelon granita, followed by an inky cup of espresso, and you know it's Venice in summer. "To me it is the best refreshment," Francesco insists. Watermelon is so Venetian. Refreshing slices of the fruit were a popular snack in the 18th century. In 1527 Pietro Aretino, a Roman visiting the city, remarked on the sale of melons in the market. "Twenty or 25 sailing boats choked with melons are lashed together to form a kind of island where people assess the quality of the melons by sniffing them and weighing them."

Purée the watermelon in a food processor, then force it through a sieve.

Mix the watermelon juice with the lemon juice and sugar to taste, mixing well to dissolve the sugar.

Spread the mixture into a metal cake pan and place in the freezer. When it becomes slushy, mix it up, then continue to freeze it, mixing it again as it begins to harden, about every 30 minutes, for about 4 hours. Serve in goblets.

Photograph on page 138.

MAKES 2 PINTS.

SIMPLE POACHED PEACHES

INGREDIENTS

1½ cups (375 g) sugar

3 cups (750 ml) water

1½ cups (375 ml) dry white wine

1 long strip lemon zest

8 ripe peaches, preferably white

Peaches in light golden syrup are the essence of summer. If you can find lush, fragrant white peaches, by all means use them. And serving them unpitted, while less convenient to eat perhaps, enhances their flavor.

Combine the sugar, water, wine, and lemon zest in a 3-quart (3-l) saucepan. Bring to a simmer and cook for 10 minutes. Add the peaches and simmer until they are just tender, about 20 minutes.

Remove from the heat and allow the peaches to cool in the syrup. When they are cool, slip off the skins. Return the peaches to the syrup and refrigerate until ready to serve.

Serve the peaches in stemmed glasses with some of the syrup poured over them.

MAKES 8 SERVINGS.

BAKED PEACHES

INGREDIENTS

14 amaretti cookies

2½ tablespoons (40 ml) amaretto liqueur

3½ tablespoons (50 g) soft unsalted butter

4 large ripe peaches

1⅔ cups (340 ml) dry white wine

Whipped cream or ice cream (optional)

The aroma of fruits in Venice is often as compelling as their lush taste. "The fragrance of ripe peaches is enhanced by baking them with a filling of amaretti," Francesco says.

Preheat the oven to 375°F (190°C). Crumble the amaretti and mix them with the liqueur and the butter.

Cut the peaches in half and remove the pits. Mound a spoonful of the amaretto mixture in the center of each.

Place the peaches, cut side up, in a baking dish. Pour the wine into the dish, place the dish in the oven, and bake 40 to 45 minutes.

Allow to cool about 30 minutes, then serve while still warm with whipped cream or ice cream on the side.

MAKES 4 SERVINGS.

FRESH PEACH TART

INGREDIENTS

1½ cups (185 g) flour

¼ teaspoon salt

10 tablespoons (160 g) cold unsalted butter,
  in small pieces

3 tablespoons (45 ml) ice water
  (approximately)

¼ cup (30 g) plain cookie crumbs

2 tablespoons (30 g) soft butter

6 ripe peaches, pitted and cut into slices
  1 inch (2.5 cm) thick

⅓ to ½ cup (90 to 125 g) sugar

The pastry for this tart is given extra flakiness by folding it several times before rolling it, similar to the way the French make puff pastry.

Combine the flour and salt. Cut in the cold butter by hand or in a food processor until the mixture is mealy. Add enough of the water, stirring lightly, just until the mixture can be gathered into a dough. Wrap it in plastic and chill it 1 hour.

Remove the dough from the refrigerator, flatten it with a rolling pin, then roll it into a rectangle ½ inch (1.3 cm) thick. Fold the rectangle like a business letter, roll it until ½ inch (1.3 cm) thick, fold it again, and refrigerate about ½ hour.

Preheat the oven to 425°F (220°C). Roll the dough to fit into a tart pan 9 inches (23 cm) in diameter. Sprinkle the crumbs over the bottom, then arrange the peach slices on top. Dot the peaches with the soft butter and sprinkle with sugar, using more or less depending on the sweetness of the fruit.

Bake 15 minutes, lower the oven temperature to 375°F (190°C), and bake about 45 minutes longer, until the dough is lightly browned and the peaches are just beginning to brown along the edges.

Remove from the oven and allow to sit for 2 to 3 hours before serving.

MAKES 8 SERVINGS.

POACHED PEARS WITH PINK PEPPERCORNS

INGREDIENTS

4 cups (1 l) dry white wine

2 cups (500 ml) water

¾ cup (185 g) sugar

2 tablespoons lightly crushed pink peppercorns

6 ripe but firm pears, peeled and cored and left whole

*P*ink peppercorns suggest nouvelle cuisine or, as it is called in Italy, nuova cucina, but in reality they have been used in Venice for many centuries. Venetian traders introduced them from East Africa and, called "grains of paradise," they were first recorded in 1214. Fanciful Venetian glass goblets set off the poached pears. Adam Tihany would serve each in a different glass.

Combine the wine, water, sugar, and peppercorns in a deep nonreactive saucepan. (Do not use a plain aluminum or iron pan.) Bring to a boil and simmer gently for 5 minutes.

Add the pears and simmer for 15 minutes.

Remove the pears from the saucepan and transfer them to a bowl. Boil down the cooking liquid until it is reduced by about half. Pour over the pears and refrigerate for at least 4 hours or overnight.

Serve the pears in deep dishes with the poaching liquid and peppercorns.

MAKES 6 SERVINGS.

Poached Pears with Pink Peppercorns and Cornmeal Brioche Bread Pudding (recipe on page 156)

CINNAMON SEMIFREDDO
WITH CHOCOLATE SAUCE

Semifreddo, meaning "half cold," is a kind of frozen mousse that is extremely popular in Italy. It is easier than ice cream to prepare because it requires no churning as it freezes. This one is made with a zabaglione base and the seasoning, cinnamon and orange, recalls the days when Venice was at the crossroads of the spice trade. "It sounds unusual, but put on the chocolate sauce and everybody loves it," Francesco says.

INGREDIENTS

9 large egg yolks

1½ cups (375 g) sugar

⅓ cup (80 ml) dry marsala

¾ teaspoon ground cinnamon

1½ tablespoons fresh lemon juice

2 tablespoons grated orange zest

½ cup (90 g) finely chopped candied (glacé) orange peel

1½ cups (375 ml) heavy (double) cream, whipped

3 tablespoons (22 g) unsweetened cocoa powder

1 cup (250 ml) water

½ cup (125 ml) light corn (or golden) syrup

4 ounces (125 g) bittersweet (dark) chocolate, chopped

6 tablespoons (90 g) unsalted butter

Select a metal bowl that will fit cradled in a saucepan without falling in. Do not use a standard double boiler because the container should have a rounded bottom. Place the egg yolks in the bowl, add ½ cup (125 g) of the sugar, and beat with a whisk or a hand-held mixer until they become frothy. Beat in the marsala.

Fill the saucepan with water to a level just below the bottom of the bowl, bring to a simmer, and place the bowl in the saucepan. Continue beating as the mixture gradually warms and keep beating until it turns light and very thick, about 10 minutes. It should be cooked enough so it is fairly warm, with steam barely beginning to rise from it, but be careful not to overheat or you will have scrambled eggs.

Remove the bowl from the heat, place it in another bowl filled with ice, and add the cinnamon. Continue beating until the mixture is cold. Beat in the lemon juice and orange zest. Fold in the orange peel and whipped cream.

Line the bottom and sides of a 10-inch (6-cup [25-cm]) loaf pan with waxed paper, allowing the paper to extend over the sides of the pan. Spoon in the semifreddo, cover with waxed paper, and freeze for at least 4 hours.

Mix the cocoa and remaining sugar together in a saucepan, add the water and corn syrup, and simmer until the mixture is smooth. Remove from the heat and stir in the chocolate, stirring until it is melted. Stir in the butter bit by bit. Set aside or refrigerate until ready to use.

To serve, unmold the semifreddo and peel off the waxed paper. Cut into slices 1 inch (2.5 cm) thick and drizzle the chocolate sauce around each slice. The dessert is best served on chilled plates.

MAKES 12 SERVINGS.

6 large egg yolks

½ cup (125 g) sugar

½ cup (125 ml) prosecco

¾ cup (180 ml) heavy (double) cream, whipped

8 fresh figs, coarsely chopped

8 whole fresh figs (optional)

FIGS WITH ZABAGLIONE

Zabaglione, that elegant creamy froth of egg yolks, sugar, and wine, is both comfort and party food. Francesco suggests that mastering the technique of whipping up zabaglione allows the cook to have a last-minute dessert on hand at all times. "You have eggs, you have sugar, and a little wine, so you put it over what fruit you have and serve it hot or chill it or even broil it to give it a nice finish." Even though plump fresh figs in season need no adornment, they become delectably lush under a mantle of zabaglione. This zabaglione is made Venetian-style with sparkling prosecco, not marsala. It can also be served with a whole fig placed in each dish.

Select a metal bowl that will fit cradled in a saucepan without falling in, to improvise a double boiler. Do not use a standard double boiler because the container should have a rounded bottom. Place the egg yolks in the bowl, add the sugar, and beat with a whisk or a hand-held mixer until they become frothy. Beat in the prosecco.

Fill the saucepan with water to a level just below the bottom of the bowl, bring to a simmer, and place the bowl in the saucepan. Continue beating as the mixture gradually warms and keep beating until it turns light and very thick, about 10 minutes. It should be cooked enough so it is fairly warm, with steam barely beginning to rise from it, but be careful not to overheat or you will have scrambled eggs.

Remove the bowl from the heat, place it in another bowl filled with ice, and continue beating until the mixture is cold. Fold in the whipped cream and refrigerate it.

Just before serving, preheat a broiler. Spread the chopped figs in 8 individual shallow baking dishes. Spread the zabaglione over the figs. Place under the broiler and broil until the top is golden brown and glazed. If desired, add whole figs before serving. Serve at once.

MAKES 8 SERVINGS.

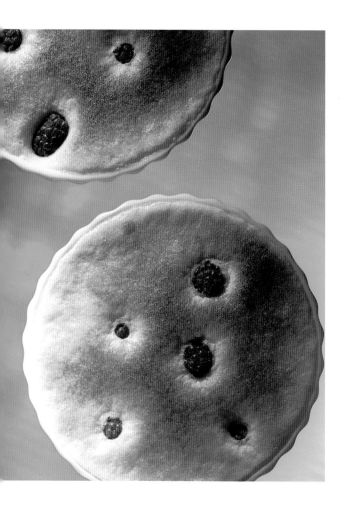

ZABAGLIONE SARAH VENEZIA

Sarah Venezia is Adam Tihany's young daughter, and this is her favorite dessert. It's simply a zabaglione that's briefly run under the broiler to brown the edges. Fresh raspberries are delicious alongside. At Remi the zabaglione is put into a star-shaped mold before broiling directly on a flameproof plate. To make the dessert at home, use shallow flameproof molds that can go directly to the table.

Place the egg yolks in a bowl, preferably unlined copper. Place the bowl over a saucepan of simmering water. It is important that the bottom of the bowl not touch the water.

With a whisk, beat the egg yolks until they are frothy, then gradually beat in the marsala and sugar. Continue beating about 5 minutes longer, until the zabaglione mixture is hot, just beginning to give off steam, very light, frothy, and thick.

Remove the bowl from the heat and continue beating until the mixture has cooled to room temperature.

To serve, divide the raspberries among 4 shallow flameproof molds, such as crème brûlée molds. A single larger mold, such as an 8-inch (20-cm) porcelain quiche dish, can be used instead. Preheat a broiler. Spread the zabaglione mixture over the raspberries into the mold or molds and place under the broiler for about 30 seconds, until the top has browned lightly. Serve at once.

MAKES 4 SERVINGS.

INGREDIENTS

8 large egg yolks

¼ cup (60 ml) sweet marsala

¼ cup (60 g) sugar

½ pint (6 ounces/180 g) fresh raspberries

1 pound (500 g) ripe but firm cherries

3 tablespoons (22 g) sliced almonds

¾ cup (185 g) sugar

1 cinnamon stick

2 cups (500 ml) valpolicella or other dry red wine

½ cup (125 ml) heavy (double) cream

2 tablespoons (30 ml) amaretto liqueur

2 tablespoons (30 g) mascarpone (see comment, page 154)

VENETIAN CHERRY COMPOTE

The food of Venice is as much about fresh fruit as it is about fish. Peaches, pears, sweet cherries, figs, grapes, and melons perfume the market. Some simple poached fruit with cookies is all it takes for dessert. "We think Americans mostly like cake, but when we serve a fruit dessert like this one at Remi, everyone loves it," Francesco admits. It calls for the sweetest, most intense cherries of the season, one of the fruits that Francesco says are as flavorful and richly perfumed in America as they are in Italy. When buying cherries, look for those with flexible green stems and pick them out one at a time so none are bruised or have soft spots.

Pit the cherries and set them aside. Place the almonds in a heavy skillet and toast over medium heat until they are lightly browned. Set aside.

Combine the sugar, cinnamon stick, and wine in a saucepan, bring to a simmer, and cook about 5 minutes. Add the cherries and cook 15 minutes longer. Transfer the cherries and their sauce to a bowl and refrigerate 1 hour or longer.

Whip the cream until soft peaks form. Fold in the amaretto and whip a few seconds longer. Fold in the mascarpone. Refrigerate until ready to serve.

Spoon the cherries and their sauce into each of 4 goblets and top with the cream. If desired, the cherries and cream can be layered. Top with the almonds and serve.

MAKES 4 SERVINGS.

TIRAMI-SU

Does anyone not know that tirami-su means "pick-me-up"? This dessert, invented in the Veneto, is almost like the Venetian version of zuppa inglese, *the Roman interpretation of English trifle. Espresso-soaked biscuits are layered with zabaglione, mascarpone, and whipped cream, then dusted with cocoa. The biscuits can be soaked in liqueur as well as espresso. "Everyone has a different way of doing it," Francesco says.*

INGREDIENTS

6 large egg yolks

¼ cup (60 g) sugar

¼ cup (60 ml) sweet marsala

1½ cups (375 g) mascarpone (see comment, page 154)

1 cup (250 ml) heavy (double) cream

1 cup (250 ml) brewed espresso, cooled

3 tablespoons (45 ml) coffee-flavored liqueur

36 savoiardi (ladyfingers), preferably homemade (recipe below)

3 tablespoons (22 g) Dutch-style cocoa powder

INGREDIENTS

4 large eggs, separated and at room temperature

½ cup (125 g) sugar

3 cups (375 g) cake flour or all-purpose flour, sifted 3 times

Beat the egg yolks in a bowl until thick. Place the bowl over, not in, a saucepan of simmering water and continue beating, gradually adding the sugar and the marsala. Beat until the mixture is as thick as softly whipped cream, about 6 minutes. Remove the bowl from the heat and continue beating until this zabaglione mixture has cooled to room temperature. Refrigerate.

Beat the mascarpone until it is smooth. Whip the cream until it forms stiff peaks, then fold it into the mascarpone. Fold in the zabaglione.

Mix the espresso with the coffee-flavored liqueur.

Line the bottom of a 9-inch (23-cm) square glass or porcelain baking dish with half the savoiardi. Brush them with half the espresso. Spoon half the zabaglione over them. Top with another layer of savoiardi, brush with the remaining espresso, and smooth the rest of the zabaglione on top. Dust the top with the cocoa sieved through a fine strainer. Refrigerate at least 1 hour before serving.

MAKES 8 TO 12 SERVINGS.

SAVOIARDI

These are simply ladyfingers, best when homemade. If you plan to buy them, try to find an Italian or French bakery instead of using the spongy supermarket variety.

Preheat the oven to 425°F (220°C). Line baking sheets with parchment paper.

Beat the egg whites until softly peaked, then beat in the sugar until the mixture makes a stiff meringue.

In a separate bowl, beat the egg yolks until they are thick and light. Fold ⅓ of the egg white mixture into the egg yolks. Sift the flour over this mixture and fold it in, then fold in the remaining egg whites.

Spoon the batter in strips about 1 × 3 inches (2.5 × 7.5 cm) onto the prepared baking sheets or, using a pastry bag with a plain ½-inch (1.3-cm) tip, pipe the batter onto the baking sheets. Bake 5 to 7 minutes, until the cookies are lightly colored. Allow them to cool before removing them from the paper.

MAKES ABOUT 5 DOZEN.

MASCARPONE RICE PUDDING

INGREDIENTS

4 ounces (125 g) long-grain rice

2 cups (500 ml) whole or low-fat milk

I vanilla bean, scraped

I cinnamon stick

2 cups (500 ml) cream or half and half
(half cream and half milk)

¾ cup (185 g) sugar

I cup (250 g) mascarpone

¼ cup slivered almonds

What might be considered nursery food is transformed into a dessert for sophisticates by adding mascarpone to it. The pudding is best if it has not been refrigerated and can be served while still slightly warm. It is a delicious foil for poached or candied fruit or fresh seasonal berries. Mascarpone is a creamy, slightly tangy fresh Italian cheese. An acceptable substitute is soft cream cheese beaten with a little yogurt.

Place the rice in a heavy saucepan, stir in the milk, vanilla bean, and cinnamon stick, bring to a simmer, and cook, stirring from time to time with a wooden spoon, until most of the milk has been absorbed, 30 to 40 minutes. Stir in all but a tablespoon of the cream and continue cooking until the rice is very tender, another 30 to 40 minutes.

Remove from the heat, stir in all but a teaspoon of the sugar, cover, and allow to cool until lukewarm, about 45 minutes. Remove the vanilla bean and cinnamon stick and stir in the mascarpone.

Mix the almonds with the reserved spoonful of cream, then toss with the reserved spoonful of sugar. Place them on a foil-lined pan in a toaster oven or 350°F (180°C) oven and toast them until they are lightly browned. Set aside.

Serve the rice pudding with a sprinkling of the nuts on top.

MAKES 4 TO 6 SERVINGS.

CORNMEAL BRIOCHE BREAD PUDDING

INGREDIENTS

1 loaf polenta brioche (recipe on page 157)

2 cups (500 ml) milk

2 cups (500 ml) heavy (double) cream

1 vanilla bean

4 large eggs

2 large egg yolks

1 cup (250 g) sugar

Butter for the baking dish

1 teaspoon ground cinnamon

*O*ld-fashioned bread pudding, a way of using leftover bread, is as typical of Venice as it is of the other frugal regions of Italy, the rest of Europe, and America. But adding some polenta to the bread dough used for the basis of the pudding gives it a distinctive character, a bit of appealing texture. "It's amazing how polenta and other foods of the poor, like beans, have become so stylish," Francesco observes.

Slice the brioche ½ inch (1.3 cm) thick and lightly toast the slices. Set aside.

Combine the milk and cream in a saucepan, add the vanilla bean, and heat just to the scalding point.

In a mixing bowl, beat the eggs and egg yolks with the sugar. Slowly whisk in the warm milk and cream mixture.

Butter a baking dish, preferably glass or ceramic.

Cut each slice of brioche in half and line the bottom of the baking dish with the slices, overlapping them slightly. Spoon about ⅓ of the egg mixture over the slices. Top with a second layer of slices and pour the remaining egg mixture evenly over them. Set aside for 30 minutes.

Preheat the oven to 300°F (150°C). Sprinkle the top of the pudding with cinnamon. Place in the oven and bake for about 1 hour, until the pudding is set. Serve while still warm with poached pears or apricots alongside if desired.

Photograph on page 146.

MAKES 8 SERVINGS.

POLENTA BRIOCHE

INGREDIENTS

1 cake fresh yeast or 1 envelope (¼ ounce/ 7 g) active dry yeast

⅓ cup (80 ml) warm heavy cream

½ cup (125 g) sugar

⅓ cup (60 g) stone-ground yellow cornmeal for polenta

10 ounces (315 g) butter (2½ sticks), softened

6 large eggs

2 teaspoons salt

5 cups (625 g) flour (approximately)

For this brioche loaf to have the proper crunchiness, it is important to use a fairly coarse-grained stone-ground cornmeal.

Dissolve the yeast in the warm cream in a bowl. Mix with 2 tablespoons (30 g) of the sugar and set aside to proof for 10 minutes. When the mixture starts becoming frothy, stir in the cornmeal. Cover and set aside in a warm place for 30 minutes.

Meanwhile, beat the remaining sugar with the butter until fluffy, either by hand or with an electric mixer. Beat in the eggs one at a time. Stir in the cornmeal mixture and salt.

Beat in the flour about ½ cup (60 g) at a time, either by hand or using an electric mixer fitted with a dough hook, to form a soft, elastic dough. The dough should be kneaded about 8 minutes.

Transfer the dough to a clean, lightly oiled bowl. Cover and allow to rise until doubled—about two hours.

Punch the dough down, divide it in half, and form each half into a rectangle 9 inches (23 cm) on one side. Roll each tightly and shape them into 2 oblong loaves. Butter 2 loaf pans, 9 × 5 × 3 inches (23 × 13 × 7.5 cm), and place the loaves in the pans, seam side down. Allow to rise until doubled, about 1½ hours.

Preheat the oven to 350°F (180°C). Bake the loaves about 30 to 40 minutes, until golden. Allow to cool completely before slicing.

MAKES 2 LOAVES.

CROCCANTE

INGREDIENTS

8 ounces (250 g) blanched almonds

1⅓ cups (310 g) sugar

⅓ cup (80 ml) water

1 baking potato, peeled and cut in
  half horizontally

Venetians taught the rest of Europe the art of working with sugar, which is the basis of this recipe for almond brittle. To make the brittle, sugar is boiled until it caramelizes, then poured over nuts on a cold surface where it then hardens to a jewellike amber with an intense caramel flavor. The croccante can be broken into pieces and eaten like candy. Crushed or pulverized, it becomes praline to sprinkle on ice cream or use to decorate cakes.

The trick of spreading the hot caramel with the cut side of a potato comes from Marcella Hazan, the cookbook author and cooking teacher who lives in Venice.

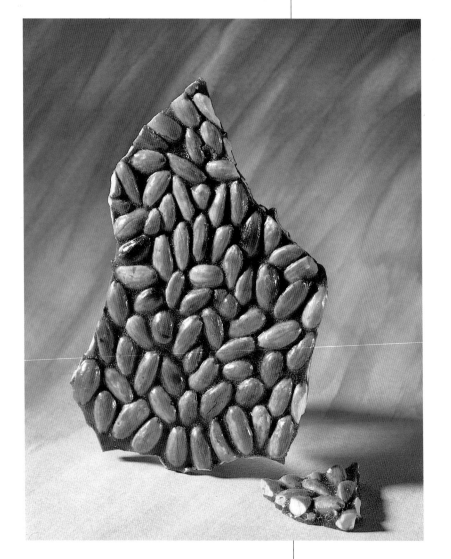

Preheat the oven to 400°F (200°C). Spread the almonds on a baking sheet and toast them 6 to 8 minutes, until they turn light brown.

Spread a sheet of foil on a work surface and oil it lightly. Spread the toasted almonds close together in a single layer on the foil.

Mix the sugar and water in a skillet, preferably nonstick. Bring to a simmer and cook over medium-high heat, tilting the pan but not stirring it, until the sugar turns pale gold. Continue cooking it, watching it closely, until it turns a rich honey color. By this time, most of the bubbling should have died down.

Immediately pour the sugar over the almonds and use the flat side of the potato to spread the caramel evenly over the nuts, until they have a thin, uniform coating of caramel. Allow to cool.

When the caramel has cooled and hardened, break it into chunks and store it in an airtight container.

MAKES ABOUT 1 POUND (500 G).

CHOCOLATE HAZELNUT BISCOTTI

INGREDIENTS

1 cup (90 g) whole hazelnuts (filberts), preferably blanched

2½ cups (310 g) flour, plus extra for work surface

½ cup (60 g) Dutch-style cocoa powder

Pinch of salt

½ teaspoon baking soda (bicarbonate of soda)

¾ teaspoon baking powder

4 large eggs

1¼ cups (310 g) sugar

1 teaspoon anise seeds

This classic crisp cookie studded with toasted hazelnuts departs from tradition with its chocolatey richness. The haunting fragrance of anise is very Venetian, however, as is the crisp, dry texture, which makes the biscotti perfect for dipping into a glass of grappa or sweet wine after dinner. "It is a cookie for dipping," Francesco says, "not a buttery cookie for eating plain."

Preheat the oven to 350°F (180°C). Spread the hazelnuts on a baking sheet and toast about 10 minutes, until lightly browned. If the hazelnuts are not blanched, toast them until the skins begin to crack, then remove them from the oven and wrap them in a clean linen or cotton towel (not terry cloth). Rub the hot nuts to remove most of the skins. Set the toasted nuts aside.

Sift the flour, cocoa powder, salt, baking soda, and baking powder together and set aside.

Beat the eggs just until they are blended in a mixing bowl with a whisk or an electric mixer. Remove 2 tablespoons (30 ml) of the egg mixture to a small dish and set aside. Beat the sugar into the remaining eggs until blended. Stir in the anise seeds, then stir in the flour mixture to form a soft dough.

Divide the dough in half and place one portion on a well-floured work surface. With floured hands, pat it into a 6-inch (15-cm) square. Scatter half the hazelnuts on the dough and press them into the surface. Roll the dough into a cylinder about 2 inches (5 cm) in diameter and 12 to 15 inches (30 to 38 cm) long. Line the baking sheet with parchment paper and place the roll of dough on it. Repeat with the remaining dough. Brush the tops of both rolls with the reserved egg.

Place in the oven and bake about 15 minutes, until firm to the touch. Transfer to a cutting board and cut on an angle into slices ½ inch (1.3 cm) thick. Return the slices to the baking sheet, standing them on edge, and return them to the oven. Bake another 20 minutes, until they are crisp and dry. Allow to cool completely before storing or serving.

MAKES ABOUT 5 DOZEN.

3¾ cups (460 g) flour

2½ teaspoons baking powder

Pinch of salt

8 ounces (250 g) unsalted butter, softened

1 cup (250 g) sugar

3 large eggs

½ cup fresh rosemary leaves

Francesco Antonucci and Adam Tihany at Florian

ROSEMARY BISCOTTI

These are not the traditional dry biscuitlike biscotti typical of northern Italy but a more buttery version. Their richness is contrasted by the fragrant and surprising addition of rosemary.

Preheat the oven to 350°F (180°C). Line a baking sheet with parchment paper.

Mix the flour, baking powder, and salt together and set aside. Beat the butter and sugar together until light and fluffy. Beat in the eggs, one at a time. Stir in the flour mixture and rosemary to form a soft dough.

Form the dough into sausage shapes about 2 inches (5 cm) in diameter. Place them on the baking sheet and bake for about 25 minutes, until they are lightly colored and fairly firm to the touch. Remove them from the oven and allow them to cool.

When the rolls have cooled, cut them on an angle into slices ¾ inch (2 cm) thick. Stand the slices on edge about ½ inch (1.3 cm) apart on the baking sheet. Use a second baking sheet if necessary. Return them to the 350°F (180°C) oven for another 20 minutes, until they have become a bit darker and firmer. Allow them to cool completely, then store them in airtight containers.

MAKES ABOUT 5 DOZEN.

"SARACEN" CORNMEAL SHORTBREAD

Venice is known for its butter cookies. Cornmeal, the basis for polenta, provides these with a delightfully crunchy texture and a rich taste. They are a variation on the Venetian fregolata, a type of shortbread cookie that is cut after it has been baked. In this recipe some buckwheat flour has been added, giving the cookies an earthy flavor. In Italy buckwheat is called grano saraceno, meaning "Saracen grain," but it is not known whether this is because the grain was introduced by the Arabs or because it is dark. In Treviso fregolata is baked to an extremely hard consistency and broken up at the table with a mallet. These cookies are tender little morsels.

INGREDIENTS

8 ounces (250 g) unsalted butter, softened

¾ cup (125 g) light brown sugar

1 cup (185 g) powdered (icing) sugar

1 cup (150 g) yellow cornmeal, preferably stone-ground

½ cup (60 g) all-purpose (plain) flour

½ cup (60 g) buckwheat flour

½ teaspoon salt

1 cup (125 g) chopped toasted blanched almonds

Shards of handblown glass in Carlo Moretti's studio on Murano

INGREDIENTS

12 ounces (375 g) bittersweet (dark) chocolate

½ cup (125 ml) heavy (double) cream

2 tablespoons (30 g) sugar

¼ cup (60 ml) grappa or brandy

½ cup (60 g) unsweetened cocoa powder

Beat the butter, brown sugar, and ¾ cup (125 g) powdered sugar together in a large bowl until smooth and light. Stir in the cornmeal, flour, buckwheat flour, and salt and mix until well blended. Mix in the almonds.

Roll the dough into 4 logs 1 inch (2.5 cm) in diameter and about 8 inches (20 cm) long. Refrigerate until firm.

Preheat the oven to 300°F (150°C). Line baking sheets with parchment paper.

Cut the logs into slices about ½ inch (1.3 cm) thick. Place the slices on the baking sheet and bake about 35 minutes, until the cookies are golden. Sift the remaining powdered sugar over the cookies once they have cooled.

MAKES ABOUT 5 DOZEN.

GRAPPA TRUFFLES

A sweet fantasy, these indescribably rich morsels. And with a glass of grappa they end a meal in luxurious Venetian style. As frugally as Venetians might eat, they do not stint on special occasions. These truffles are worthy of such an occasion. The very best bittersweet chocolate is necessary for this recipe.

Chop the chocolate fine and place it in a heatproof bowl.

In a small saucepan, mix the cream and sugar together, bring to a boil, stir, then pour over the chocolate. Add the grappa or brandy and allow the mixture to stand about 5 minutes, to melt the chocolate. Mix until smooth. Allow the mixture to cool to room temperature, then refrigerate about 2 hours, until it is fairly firm.

Using a melon baller, scoop small rounds of the chocolate mixture, then roll them lightly in your fingertips to make them smooth. Set them on a sheet of waxed paper on a baking sheet and return them to the refrigerator.

Roll the finished truffles in cocoa powder and refrigerate again until ready to serve.

MAKES ABOUT 5 DOZEN.

WHITE CHOCOLATE TRUFFLES WITH PISTACHIOS

INGREDIENTS

12 ounces (375 g) white chocolate, chopped

2 tablespoons (30 g) unsalted butter, in small pieces

⅓ cup (80 ml) heavy (double) cream

2 tablespoons (30 ml) orange liqueur (Curaçao, Triple Sec)

2 cups (200 g) unsalted shelled pistachios

6 ounces (185 g) bittersweet (dark) chocolate, chopped

This is a Carnevale masque of a confection, its dark, nut-encrusted exterior enrobing creamy white chocolate. While not technically demanding to prepare, it calls for time and patience.

Combine the white chocolate and butter in a metal bowl.

In a small saucepan, bring the cream and liqueur to a boil, pour over the chocolate and butter, and mix well to blend. Place the bowl in a larger bowl of ice and allow it to cool 15 to 20 minutes, stirring it frequently as it cools. Do not allow it to harden.

When the chocolate mixture has cooled, beat it until it is light and fluffy.

Transfer the mixture to a pastry bag and, using a plain tip with a ¼-inch (6-mm) opening, pipe small round truffles onto a baking sheet. Place them in the refrigerator until they harden, about 2 hours.

Toast the pistachios by heating them in a dry skillet or spreading them on a pan in a 350°F (180°C) oven or toaster oven. Allow them to cool, then chop them fairly fine by pulsing in a food processor. Spread the pistachios on a plate.

Melt the bittersweet chocolate in the top of a double boiler and transfer it to a small bowl.

Working quickly, dip the chilled white chocolate truffles one at a time in the bittersweet chocolate, then roll in the chopped nuts. Return to the refrigerator to harden.

MAKES ABOUT 5 DOZEN.

An assortment of Venetian cookies— "golosezi"—including biscotti, shortbreads, truffles.

An array of colorful Venetian drinks; from left to right, spriss, sgroppino, Tiziano, Bellini

D·R·I·N·K·S & W·I·N·E

Venice has more in the way of fanciful, colorful libations than any other city in Italy. Giuseppe Cipriani, the now legendary restaurateur-hotelier, contributed his share, inventing the Bellini, a mixture of sparkling prosecco and the juice of white peaches named in the honor of the 15th-century Venetian artist, and the Tiziano, a kir-like mixture of sweet red grape juice and white wine. Spritz, simply wine and sparkling water, or the more complex spriss, best described as a cross between a kir and a martini, along with the now fashionable sgroppino made with lemon sorbet, prosecco, and vodka, are some others.

The most popular drink in Venice, however, remains the ubiquitous glass of white wine, or *ombra*. The name *ombra* means "shadow" and refers to a time, during the late 14th century, when wine stalls on St. Mark's Square would move their outdoor tables into the shadow, or *ombra*, of the Campanile so their patrons could enjoy a glass of wine in the shade instead of the hot sun. In the narrow streets near the Rialto, branching from the Fondaco dei Tedeschi, dim little wine bars pour the *ombra* to wash down a bite of cicchetti for marketgoers in the morning.

The wine in the *ombra* glass is light, hardly memorable, and from the region, probably made from gargenaga,

the grape that produces Soave in the designated area near Verona. Some other traditional grape varieties like vespaiolo compete with newer plantings of pinot bianco and pinot grigio in the Breganze area near Vicenza. Tocai is grown in the hills to the north of Venice.

A wide variety of other dry white wines comes not only from the Veneto but also from Friuli and Alto Adige. There always seems to be a certain harmony about the wine-making traditions of a region and the way they complement the food. It is therefore hardly surprising that an area in which seafood dominates would specialize in white wine.

Friuli produces the popular pinot grigio, as well as trendy grapes like sauvignon blanc and chardonnay. Crisp tocai, fragrant riesling and traminer, and herbaceous verduzzo are also cultivated in Friuli. The mountainous Alto Adige region bordering Austria and Switzerland closely resembles Alsace as a wine region, with similar grape varieties like riesling, sylvaner, pinot bianco, müller-thurgau, traminer, and muscat under cultivation. All these regions produce excellent dry, sparkling prosecco, the champagne of Venice.

Several kinds of sweet white wines are made, notably the strong, honey-colored malvasia and the rich, rare picolit from Friuli. From the Veneto there is the slightly raisiny

At the Maculan winery, a wine cellar (above) and a vineyard (below)

recioto di Soave, made from partly dried grapes, and torcolato, an intense sweet wine made from grapes twisted on their branches into great hanks and left to dry in attics.

The Veneto is known for its popular Bardolino and valpolicella, light-bodied young red wines. When partly dried, the grapes that make valpolicella are pressed to make a strong, intense wine called amarone, also known as recioto della valpolicella. Smooth red wines from merlot and cabernet sauvignon are produced mainly in Friuli. Some are also produced in the Veneto. Cabernet franc and refosco are also grown in this area.

After dinner the Venetian will pour a glass of clear, fiery grappa. In the mountains, grappa may also be a morning's winter warmer. But in the city the grappas have become smooth and refined, as befits their elegant, often fanciful containers, expressions of the Venetian glassblower's art.

Traditionally, grappa is made from the pomace left from making wine. "Leave it to the Italians to figure out a way to make cheap leftovers into something rare and expensive," Francesco observes. But a new wave of grappa producers now makes varieties that are smoother and more aromatic by using pomace that has been only gently pressed. Varietal grappas are popular now, as are distillates of grapes called *ùe*. Eaux de vie distilled from other fruits and even oddities like tea roses and wild olives are another after-dinner specialty of the region.

A traditional Venetian saying goes like this: *Chi no ghe piase el vin, Dio ghe toga l'acqua,* "God will take water away from him who does not like wine."

SPRISS

INGREDIENTS

1 green olive, with pit

2 tablespoons (30 ml) Campari

4 ounces (125 ml) dry white wine

4 ounces (125 ml) club soda

"This is a typical Sunday morning drink in Venice, sort of a cross between a kir and a martini," Francesco says. He attributes the recipe to some of the new ideas about food and drink that have become popular in Venice recently. "Venice is so touristic it's impossible for us not to learn new things all the time," he adds. Although Francesco insists the olive is essential to the drink, it's also fine without it.

Skewer the olive with a toothpick and place it in a champagne glass. Add the Campari, then the wine.

Add the soda and serve immediately.

MAKES 1 SERVING.

BELLINI

INGREDIENTS

1 cup chilled fresh or frozen peach purée, preferably white peach

1 bottle chilled prosecco, very dry sparkling wine, or champagne

A cocktail that has become famous throughout the world, the Bellini was named by Giuseppe Cipriani in 1948 in honor of an exhibition of the 15th-century Venetian artist's works. Supposedly the drink was invented by Cipriani in the 1930s and, unnamed, became the most popular cocktail at Harry's Bar. Purists insist it be made only with the purée of white peaches, but people take liberties these days.

Place 2 tablespoons of the peach purée in the bottom of 8 champagne flutes or wine glasses.

Slowly pour the prosecco or other sparkling wine into the glasses and serve.

MAKES 8 COCKTAILS.

SGROPPINO

INGREDIENTS

1 cup (250 g) lemon sorbet

2 cups (500 ml) prosecco

¼ cup (60 ml) chilled grappa

4 sprigs fresh rosemary

Sgroppino is a newly fashionable after-dinner drink that can double as dessert. "In Venice it's made with vodka, but why not grappa?" Francesco asks. Be sure to use top-quality lemon sorbet—an ice, not a sherbet—and the bone-dry Venetian sparkling wine prosecco to make sgroppino.

Place all the ingredients except the rosemary in a chilled metal bowl. Using a whisk, beat them together by hand quickly.

Spoon the mixture into champagne glasses and serve at once, garnished with sprigs of rosemary.

MAKES 4 SERVINGS.

TIZIANO

INGREDIENTS

1 cup chilled red grape juice

1 bottle chilled prosecco, very dry sparkling wine, or champagne

Titian, the Venetian painter known for his use of red, lends his name to this rosy mixture of red grape juice and sparkling wine. It is another drink named by Giuseppe Cipriani. When made with strawberry purée, it's called a Rossini.

Pour the grape juice into 8 champagne flutes or wine glasses.

Slowly pour in the prosecco or other sparkling wine and serve.

MAKES 8 COCKTAILS.

Flasks of grappas from the Veneto and Friuli

ENTERTAINING, V·E·N·E·T·I·A·N S·T·Y·L·E

*V*enetian life reflects a passion for drama and display. The glitter, improbable color, and arabesque detail of the facades along the canals and *campos* reappear in aspects of the daily routine, in the frill of purple radicchio arrayed in the market, the baroque curl of glazed cookies and pastel sweets in pastry shops, the serpentine lines of candlesticks and stemware, and the shimmer of silks and velvets draped at the windows.

When Venetians entertain the events are embellished by their delight in decoration, tempting the eye as well as the palate. The Venetian table charms the imagination and gives substance to dreams and romance.

"You see the unbelievable glassware, the incredible delicacy of the design, and you think you will never be able to pick it up and actually drink," said Adam Tihany as he made his way along a narrow street on Murano, the island of the glass factories. "But then someone pours some wine or some grappa into this amazing pink or blue thing and before you know it you are part of the fantasy."

Venetian glass—so delicate because it is made like ancient glass, improbably thin without lead and responding to the whim of the glassblower—is meant to be used. For the connoisseur who shudders at the sight of gaudy tourist shops filled with glass gondolas there are dealers who sell breathtaking antiques as well as new designs wrought with astonishing artistry. These glasses, blown like the merest bubbles and trimmed with the flick of the wrist as molten globs emerge from fiery furnaces, exemplify the craft as much today as hundreds of years ago.

Designers like Carlo Moretti have transformed tradition into the contemporary brilliance of a shallow coupe poised on a bright teardrop of a base or the simple fine swirl of a flute for prosecco. "What amazes me is that this craft is not stuck in the past," Tihany said. "People like Moretti are keeping Venice alive so it is not just a beautiful but irrelevant museum."

Like Tihany himself, the Venetian uses such glassware, as well as creamy ceramics, exquisitely wrought silver, and fine silks. Handworked crocheted lace and handkerchief linen made and sold at the Jesurum showroom near the

Antique glasses at a dealer's warehouse on Murano

Glassware poised on a window ledge in Carlo Moretti's studio on Murano

Bridge of Sighs cover tables with proud finery and edge the napkins, just as they did centuries ago. Lacemakers, always women, cluster on wooden chairs in sun-drenched ateliers on the colorful island of Burano, giving new vigor to a delicate craft that, a few decades ago, was threatened with extinction as modern tastes abandoned handmade goods for mass-produced items. But renewed appreciation has increased the ranks of those adept at the craft today.

Similarly threatened, the ancient technique of marbling paper was revived by Alberto Valese in the early 1970s. Like the sugar and the spice trade, this craft came to Venice in the 15th century from the Far East in the baggage of Arab traders. The magical, swirling, dappled patterns of color, often flecked with gold, are again all the rage on paper and fabric. Or perhaps the Venetian will choose the hand-printed papers of Piazzesi in dense, muted colors to summon guests to a dinner party, thank other hosts, assign places at table, or identify their books.

Radiant, lustrous hand-printed silks and velvets inspired by the Renaissance upholster the chairs and richly frame the windows in the dining room, not only in Venetian palazzi but in stylish salons around the globe, residences that are also furnished and adorned with finely forged or cast bronze and copper.

Venetian woodworkers create and repair fine furniture, restoring marquetry and buffing warm, glowing finishes. And there remain just two studios that make the oddly shaped yet perfectly tuned *forcola*, the polished dark wood oarlock on which a gondolier depends. This craft has been passed along from father to son for generations, just like the gondolier tradition. The gondola, Venice's equivalent of the horse and carriage mostly for the amusement of tourists, is a livelihood today for some 400 gondoliers.

As each gondolier has his style of rowing, adjusted to the weight of his sleek and subtly asymmetrical boat, so must his *forcola* suit him, the way a glove fits a pitcher's hand. The maker of a *forcola*, a uniquely Venetian artisan, uses no set pattern, but carves and sands the shape instinctively. And the gondolier removes his personal oarlock and takes it with him every time he parks his craft.

There are also mosaic studios, beadmakers, and the makers of the mysterious often bird-beaked masks for Carnevale.

"Venice may look like a stage set," Tihany said, "but all around, in people's homes, the things that tourists gaze at in shop windows are actually used every day."

The use of these dramatic accessories often involves a gathering. Venetians love to entertain. Any occasion, or none at all, is an excuse to assemble, drink, and eat. It may be a supper after the theater, a Sunday lunch on a terrace, a small dinner, cocktails, or great gala costume feasts for Carnevale. The Venetian day is punctuated by meals and snacks, from the *ombra* or glass of white wine in late morning to the final grappa late at night.

If they are not creating a market-fresh repast with friends at home Venetians meet in their favorite restaurants where everyone dines on the grilled seafood, the risotto or

Dyes and rollers, shown here, are used to embellish leather bindings.

Block-printed and hand-marbled papers on display at Legatoria Piazzesi

The showroom of Jesurum, in a former convent

may discover an old piece of lace in a flea market to throw over a plain cloth to dress the table. Or replace severe white candles in your candlesticks with twisted gold or pastel ones. Or tie napkins with gauzy iridescent ribbons meant for gift-wrap.

Pay attention to the color of the food on the plate and do not hesitate to startle guests with its vibrancy. But above all, be inspired to offer finesse and quality, regardless of how simple the occasion.

Venice may look like an illusion, but for centuries it has been filled with cooks and craftsmen who take pride in the refinement of their unique products. It maintains this sensibility to this day, making it the essence of Venetian taste.

To sum it up Tihany says: "You take the fantasy and make it real."

polenta, and the cookies that are served at every other restaurant. And given a chance to escape to the countryside, these waterborne souls delight in a picnic.

No matter what the place or the occasion, the Venetian insists that entertaining must include the ultimate in style and quality.

How can anyone who does not inhabit this magnificent island kingdom participate in the Venetian sensibility? Some of Venice's finest products, like the glassware and fabrics, are sold elsewhere. But Venetian style requires more than the mere purchase of Venetian goods. One must add a playful willingness to indulge in tastes, shapes, color, and imagination. As Tihany said, proffering some tiny raw razor clams, "Try some—dare to be Venetian."

You will not find the clams anywhere else. But you

Saverio Pastor making a **forcola,** *the gondolier's oarlock*

Here are some suggested menus for entertaining Venetian-style. They are based on the lunches, dinners, picnics, and parties photographed in Venice and shown in this chapter. In some instances the quantities in the original recipes have to be increased or reduced as indicated.

On Murano, sculptor Luciano Vistosi's creative vision materializes in shimmering glass (right). Dark secrets glow from within the deep green and black of once-molten material that has been fixed in sinuous shapes or assembled in mirror-finished hard-edge construction. A buffet (above) that Adriana Vistosi assembled in their sunny, whitewashed home was a forthright, simple contrast to her husband's art. As we sipped wine from cobalt-blue goblets, Luciano told of the glassblower's lunch, a Christmas Eve tradition that dates from the Middle Ages. The furnaces are shut down, fresh eels are put in the cooling ovens to roast, and each glassmaster and his team of workers offers a dish to the group. Glass trumpets herald the wives to the party and a special goblet is presented for the best dish. Glassblower's chicken, roasted in the ashes, often wins.

*F*rom their terrace perched atop a carefully restored house in Cannaregio, a district that looks out over the lagoon toward the cemetery islet of San Michele and the glassblowing island of Murano and includes the Jewish ghetto area, the Hazans see the dome of the church of Santi Giovanni e Paolo. From their sheltered spot, they pour carefully selected wines of Victor's choosing to complement Marcella's superb cooking.

MARCELLA AND VICTOR HAZAN'S LUNCHEON ON THE TERRACE FOR FOUR

Arugula Salad with Parmesan Cheese and
Walnut-Olive Dressing (page 36)
Basic Soft Polenta (pages 68–69, halve)
Pan-Roasted Quail (page 129, double)
Watermelon Granita (page 141, halve)
Wine: Valpolicella, preferably from a
single vineyard

DINNER FOR TWO AT CAFFÈ ORIENTALE

Clams (or Mussels) Venetian Style (page 44)
Risotto with Wild Mushrooms (page 60, halve)
Red Snapper with Red Onion, Pignoli, and
  Raisins ("In Saor") (page 110)
Rosemary Biscotti (page 160)
Sgroppino (page 168, halve)
Wine: Chardonnay

A COCKTAIL PARTY IN A PALAZZO FOR SIXTEEN TO TWENTY

*T*his is a fantasy. Whether or not a palazzo provides the setting, many of Venice's— and Francesco's—delectable little savories are suited to such a gathering.

Venetian Cocktails and wines
Sage Potato Chips (page 26, triple)
Cicchetti Olives (page 28, double)
Cicchetti Polenta with Onions and Sausage
  (page 30, triple)
Rosemary Grissini (page 31)
Venetian Pizza (page 32, double)
Sweet-and-Sour Shallots (page 39, double)
Country Terrine (page 49)

*I*n the morning the Rialto is an invitation to cook. The shimmering array of fish and sea creatures, bright vegetables and fruits, sacks of grain, and snowy cheeses is hard to resist. As it is for many home cooks, shopping at the Rialto is a daily routine for Sandro Scarpa from the Caffè Orientale, an out-of-the-way restaurant not far from the market that is typical of Venice's small yet alluring places. This menu is loosely inspired by the food at Caffè Orientale, where seafood is the focus. But it does not depend strictly on the Rialto, as is evident from the red snapper, a fish from Florida whose closest Venetian equivalent might be sea bream. It calls for whatever is market fresh at the moment and is given as an example, a suggestion of the possibilities.

*V*enetians take to the outdoors for dining whenever they can. The occasion might be a family gathering of many generations at the restored farmhouse in Mestre owned by Francesco Antonucci's cousins, or a table set among the vines of the Maculan winery near Breganze (left). An outdoor spread invariably features basic, informal dishes that need not be eaten hot—or chilled—but that always depend on market-fresh ingredients whose flavors are especially delicious.

FRANCESCO'S FESTIVE DINNER PARTY FOR TEN TO TWELVE

Goat Cheese with Tomato Sauce (page 34)

Tuna Ravioli with Ginger Marco Polo
    (page 81, double)

Mashed Parmesan Potatoes (page 98, double)

Zucchini in Umido (page 101, triple)

Roast Racks of Lamb (page 134)

Cinnamon Semifreddo with Chocolate Sauce
    (page 147)

Grappa Truffles (page 161)

Wines: Prosecco, Refosco, Picolit

A dinner at the rustic table (below) just steps from the kitchen at Remi–New York is inevitably a gathering of good friends, a joyous event to savor some of Francesco's specialties.

Remi restaurant in New York

DINNER ON THE TERRACE AT THE CIPRIANI FOR FOUR

Stuffed Zucchini Flowers (page 48)

Risotto with Shrimp and Radicchio (page 61)

Vegetable Casserole (page 103)

Guinea Hen with Black Pepper Sauce
    (page 125, triple)

Zabaglione Sarah Venezia (page 150)

Bellinis (page 167)

Wines: Tocai Friuliano, Amarone

The Cipriani (above) on the island of Giudecca, one of the world's great hostelries, was founded by Giuseppe Cipriani, who created Harry's Bar. Minutes from San Marco by water taxi, it is a restorative, lushly planted retreat, especially in summer. And it offers a magical view of Venice to those dining on its spacious terrace, enjoying cosmopolitan renditions of Venetian cuisine.

*F*ar from the Grand Canal the Venetian spirit can flourish. Venice is everywhere in the Mariottis' small New York apartment, in the glassware, carafes, and fanciful glass Venetian "candy" on the table, the collection of paintings on the walls and the food. With no Rialto market close at hand there are shrimp in place of scampi and the artichokes could be smaller. But the color, freshness, and flavor of Venice are present for guests to savor.

*T*he Luna Baglione, in a 14th-century building newly restored, provided an elegant setting for Carnevale's pre-Lenten feast (above). The finery in the dining salon, with its silk walls and tables draped in magnificent lace, was matched by the costumes on the guests and the vibrant colors and flavors on the plates: black risotto, rosy tuna, golden polenta, and a fanciful tirami-su.

Remi—New York

LIST OF SOURCES IN VENICE

(The city code for telephoning Venice is 41.)

Ceramics and Tableware

Camuffo, Rio Terrà Nomboli,
2799 San Polo, tel. 71-93-76.

Il Quadrifoglio, 5576 San Lio,
tel. 522-28-22.

Padnacco, Mercerie, 231 San Marco,
tel. 522-37-04.

Fabrics

Adriana da Venezia, 2793 Dorsoduro,
tel. 522-15-35.

Delphos, Calle Larga 22 Marzo,
2403 San Marco, tel. 522-92-81.

Luigi Bevilacqua, 1320 Santa Croce,
tel. 72-15-66.

Norelene, Campo San Maurizio,
2606 San Marco, tel. 523-73-05.

Rubelli, 3977 San Marco, tel. 521-64-11.

Glassware

Archimede Seguso, Fondamenta Serenella
18, Murano, tel. 73-90-48.

Barovier e Toso, Fondamenta Vetrai 28,
Murano, tel. 73-90-49.

Carlo Moretti, Fondamenta Manin 3,
Murano, tel. 73-92-17; L'Isola
(retail shop near San Marco),
Campo San Moisè, 1468 San Marco,
tel. 523-19-73.

EOS Design nel Vetro, Calle Vivarini 5,
Murano, tel. 527-44-56.

Linea Vetro, Fondamenta Vetrai 68,
Murano, tel. 527-44-55.

Venini, Piazzetta dei Leoncini, 314 San
Marco, tel. 522-40-45; Fondamenta
Vetrai 50, Murano, tel. 73-99-55.

Lace, Tablecloths

Cenerentola, Calle dei Saoneri 2721,
tel. 523-20-06.

Jesurum, Ponte della Canonica 4310,
San Marco, tel. 520-61-77.

Maria Mazzaron, Fondamenta
dell'Osmarin, 4970 San Provolo,
Castello, tel. 522-13-92.

Ottocento, Calle Racchetta, 3792
Cannaregio, tel. 528-50-25.

Masks

Mondo Novo Maschere, Ponte dei Pugni,
3063 Dorsoduro, tel. 528-73-44.

Paper

Alberto Valese-Ebru, Calle della Fenice
1920, tel. 528-63-02; Salizada
San Samuele 3135, tel. 520-09-21.

Legatoria Piazzesi, Santa Maria
del Giglio, 2511 San Marco,
tel. 522-12-02.

Olbi, Calle della Mondola, 3653
San Marco, tel. 528-50-25.

Polliero, Frari, 2995 San Polo,
tel. 528-51-30.

Silver and Bronze

Aureliano Visinoni, 6145 Cannaregio,
tel. 523-55-36.

Maria Grazia Moroni, 2863 San Polo,
tel. 520-33-99.

Sfriso, Campo San Tomà, 2849 San Polo,
tel. 522-35-58.

Valese-Founder, Calle Fiubera,
793 San Marco, tel. 522-72-82.

Woodwork

Livio de Marchi, 1831 San Marco,
tel. 522-81-11; San Samuele,
3157A San Marco, tel. 528-69-53.

OTHER SOURCES FOR VENETIAN PRODUCTS

Avventura
    463 Amsterdam Avenue
    New York, NY 10024
    tel. (212) 769-2510
    glassware and ceramics

Bergdorf Goodman
    754 Fifth Avenue
    New York, NY 10019
    tel. (212) 753-7300
    glassware

Claremont Furnishings/Fabrics Ltd.
    29 Elystan Street
    London SW3 3NT
    tel. (71) 581-9575
    fabrics

The Conran Shop
    Michelin House
    81 Fulham Road
    London SW3 6RD
    tel. (71) 589-7401
    household furnishings

Dîners en Ville
    27 rue de Varenne
    75007 Paris
    tel. (1) 42 22 78 33
    glassware

Diva
    97 rue du Bac
    75007 Paris
    tel. (1) 45 48 95 39
    Murano glass

Gardner & Barr Inc.
    213 East 60th Street
    New York, NY 10022
    tel. (212) 752-0555
    antique glassware

Harrod's
    Knightsbridge
    London SW1
    tel. (71) 730-1234
    household furnishings

Muriel Grateau Boutique
    29 rue de Valois
    75001 Paris
    tel. (1) 40 20 90 30
    glassware and ceramics

San Marco Galerie
    25 bis rue Benjamin Franklin
    75016 Paris
    tel. (1) 45 53 56 72
    Murano glass

Tiffany & Co.
    727 Fifth Avenue
    New York, NY 10022
    tel. (212) 755-8000
    25 Old Bond Street
    London
    tel. (71) 409-2790
    Also in Beverly Hills, Boston,
    Chicago, Costa Mesa, Dallas, Detroit,
    Hawaii, Houston, Palm Beach, San
    Diego, San Francisco, Troy (Mich.),
    Washington; also in Europe in Berlin,
    Florence, Frankfurt; and in Asia in
    Hong Kong, Singapore, Tokyo.
    glassware

Véronèse
    184 boulevard Haussmann
    75008 Paris
    tel. (1) 45 62 67 67
    lamps, lighting

Villeroy & Boch Tableware, Ltd.
    41 Madison Avenue
    New York, NY 10016
    tel. (212) 683-1747
    household furnishings

DINING IN VENICE

Restaurants

Al Covo, Campiello della Pescaria 3968, Castello, tel. 522-38-12. Small, with superb fish, good wine list.

Alla Colomba, Piscina della Frezzeria 1665, San Marco, tel. 522-11-75. Luxurious, with modern painting collection.

Antica Locanda Montin, Fondamenta di Borgo 1147, Dorsoduro, tel. 522-71-51. Grilled fish, historic.

Caffè Orientale, 2426 San Polo, tel. 71-98-04. Seafood specialties, Josef Hoffman–style setting.

Cipriani, Zitelle 10, Giudecca, tel. 520-77-44. Classic, international, outdoor terrace.

Corte Sconta, Calle del Pestrin 3886, Castello, tel. 522-70-24. Informal, some unusual fish dishes.

Da Fiore, Calle dello Scaleter 2202, San Polo, tel. 72-13-08. Simple setting with excellent food.

Harry's Bar, Calle Vallaresso 1323, San Marco, tel. 528-53-31. Famous, chic and expensive, excellent food.

Ponte del Diavolo, Torcello, tel. 73-04-01. Airy, rustic, excellent food.

Ristorante Canova, Luna Hotel Baglioni, Calle Larga Ascensione, 1243 San Marco, tel. 528-98-40. Formal setting with creative Venetian cuisine.

Riviera, 1473 Dorsoduro, tel. 522-76-21. Fried fish, friendly, outdoor terrace.

Cafés and Wine Bars

Do Mori, San Polo 401/403, tel. 522-54-01. Typical wine bar near the Rialto.

Do Spade, Calle Do Spade 860, tel. 521-05-74. Wine bar, good cicchetti.

Florian, Piazza San Marco, 56-59 San Marco, tel. 528-69-74. Historic.

Harry's Dolci, Fondamenta San Biagio 773, Giudecca, tel. 522-48-44. Light food, sweets, and famous Harry's Bar drinks.

Quadri, Piazza San Marco, 120 San Marco, tel. 522-21-05. Historic.

REMI RESTAURANTS

Remi–New York
125 West 53rd Street
New York, NY 10019
Tel. (212) 581-4242

Rialto Room (lunch and private parties)
144 West 54th Street
Tel. (212) 757-7610

Remi To Go
Atrium, 145 West 53rd Street
Tel. (212) 581-7115

Remi Santa Monica
1451 Third Street Promenade
Santa Monica, California 90401
    Classic restaurant in historic, newly restored hotel.
Tel. (310) 393-6545

Remi Mexico City
Andres Bello No. 10 P.B.
Col. Polanco
Mexico City, D.F.
Tel. (5) 282-0062

Remi Tel Aviv
King David Tower
Hayarkon Street
Tel Aviv, Israel
Tel. (3) 251-111

G·E·N·E·R·A·L I·N·D·E·X

I·N·D·E·X O·F R·E·C·I·P·E·S